ACUA
Underwater Archaeology
Proceedings
2019

edited by

David Ball and Christopher Horrell

An Advisory Council on Underwater Archaeology Publication

2019 © Advisory Council on Underwater Archaeology

Made possible in part through the support of the
Society for Historical Archaeology

Cover Image: Far West, 1996 Riverboats Series; Avery Dennison, Photogravure

Forward iii

Contributing Authors

Geophyiscal Investigations to Locate the Wreck of an iconic Upper Missouri River
Mountain Packet Steamboat 1
    Douglas D. Scott, Bert Ho, Sadie Dasovich, Steve Dasovich, and David L.
    Conlin

Coming in with a Tide, Going out with a Forklift: The Spring Break Shipwreck Project 7
    Allyson Ropp

Hull Remains of the Spring Break Wreck, a Nineteenth-Century Shipwreck Washed
Ashore at Ponte Vedra Beach, Florida..13
    Chuck Meide

A Square Peg in a Round Hole: Wood Analysis from the Spring Break Wreck 23
    Brendan Burke & Lee Newsom

Happy Anniversary! We Didn't Get You A Card but We Found a Lot of Ship: Revisiting
the Anniversary Wreck..33
    Silvana Kreines, Chuck Meide, Megan Bebee

Heritage Monitoring Underwater: Launching the Submerged Heritage Monitoring
Scouts Florida Program 42
    Rachael Kangas, Jeffrey Moates, Brenda Altmeier, Sara Ayers-Rigsby

30 Years Later: Revisiting the 1733 *San Pedro* and *San Felipe* Shipwrecks in the Florida Keys 49
    Samuel I. Haskell, Tori L. Galloway, Matthew Lawrence, Charles D. Beeker,
    Kirsten M. Hawley

In Situ Digital Documentation of the 1559 Emanuel Point Shipwrecks 56
    Micah B. Minnocci & Hunter W. Whitehead

Rebuilding the Past: Digitizing Ship Lines into 3D Models 62
    Arik J. K. Bord

Identifying Aircraft Artifacts Ex Situ: The Life History of an F4U Corsair 69
    Hunter W. Whitehead

An Account of Stone Anchors: A Study of Northern Shoreline of the Persian Gulf 77
    Sorna Khakzad & Ali Moosaie

Survey Says…:
Using Archaeological Lenses and Conservation Assessment Tools to Influence Curation 87
    Hannah Fleming & Lesley Haines

2020 SHA Calendar Art Award Winners 95

Foreword

Making the Most of Opportunities

This year's conference coincided with the 50th meeting of the annual Conference on Underwater Archaeology. First held in St. Paul, Minnesota, in 1963, this conference highlights the work and efforts of underwater archaeologists from around the world. From its beginnings, the Advisory Council on Underwater Archaeology (and its' predecessor, the Council on Underwater Archaeology) have endeavored to publish a collection of underwater-related papers presented at, what is now referred to as, the annual SHA Conference on Historical and Underwater Archaeology. Having missed only a few publications in its early years when the meetings were biennial, and a brief hiatus from 2000 through 2006, this issue marks the 13th consecutive publication of the outstanding work conducted by our colleagues since 2007. While the 2019 Proceedings may not include as many contributions as previous Proceedings, it nonetheless continues the tradition of highlighting the quality and scholarship of the current field of maritime archaeology.

The theme of this year's conference, Making the Most of Opportunities: Education, Training, and Experiential Learning, turned out to be apropos. Bookended between the 2018 conference in New Orleans and the 2020 conference in Boston, expectations were tempered regarding the total number of conference attendees and presentations for the 2019 conference in St. Charles, Missouri. And the furlough of federal government employees helped keep those expectations in check. Nonetheless, those that made it to the 2019 conference experienced the small town charm and history of St. Charles and enjoyed a conference that was intimate, warm, and reminiscent of the early conferences. The smaller numbers also increased opportunities for networking, as well as catching up with old friends and making new ones.

Of the 342 total submissions for the 2019 Conference, about 25% focused on maritime archaeology. Five of the 22 organized symposia highlighted maritime research, including a session by the Lighthouse Maritime Archaeology Program (LAMP) on the Spring Break Wreck; a two-part session on research at the Richard Steffy Ship Reconstruction Laboratory; a public outreach session on Getting People Engaged with their Maritime History; a symposium on maritime heritage of the Great Lakes; and a session on aviation archaeology; 28 additional maritime papers were incorporated into other themed or general sessions. Three of the 17 panel discussions, six of 30 posters, and two of five roundtable lunches featured maritime themes and rounded out the program.

Just over half of the papers included in this year's Proceedings focus on shipwrecks from Florida, yet the collection as a whole highlights the general conference theme of opportunities for education, training, and experiential learning, and provides a good assortment of the various offerings presented at the 2019 Conference. The papers also provide a range of contributions from established professionals, students, and up and coming professionals. The first paper, by Scott et al., provides a synopsis of survey efforts along the lower Missouri River to identify the remains of the legendary mountain packet *Far West*, a Missouri River steamboat that played a role in the 1876 Battle of the Little Bighorn. Keeping with the Conference theme of making the most of opportunities, *Far West* is also featured on the cover of this year's Proceedings.

The next four papers from LAMP demonstrate the important contributions that organization regularly makes to the SHA Conference and the Proceedings. Three contributions from the researchers at LAMP (Ropp, Meide, and Burke and Newsom), focus on what has come to be known as the "Spring Break Wreck." These papers conveniently tie in with the 2019 Conference theme of making the most of opportunities and provide an excellent example of how a large section of hull remains from a 19th-century shipwreck that washed up overnight onto Ponte Verde Beach can be used as a tool to educate the public on the importance of maritime archaeology while making a lasting contribution to the maritime history of St. Augustine, Florida. The fourth LAMP entry, by Krienes et al., highlights the ongoing documentation of another "shipwreck of opportunity," the Anniversary Wreck, which was discovered during the 450th anniversary celebration of the city of St. Augustine.

The following two papers by Kangas, et al., and Haskell et al., underscore opportunities for education and public involvement with maritime heritage. Kangas, et al., share information on the Florida Public Archaeology Network's (FPAN) Submerged Heritage Monitoring Scout (SHMS) public outreach program. This program teaches interested divers how to help monitor underwater cultural heritage throughout Florida. While Haskell et al., summarize Indiana University's thirty-year efforts of documenting and monitoring two shipwrecks in the Florida Keys.

The next two papers consider the application of technology and computer software as a tool to help document and analyze shipwreck sites. Minnocci's and Whitehead's paper on the use of photogrammetry on two of the Emanuel Point shipwrecks from Pensacola Bay, Florida, provide just a sample of the number of papers presented at this year's Conference on the integration of photogrammetry as a tool to enhance documentation of both underwater and terrestrial sites. Bord's paper, which was part of the double session of the Richard Steffy Lab at Texas A&M University, evaluates the efficacy of 3D modeling software as a way of developing ship lines plans. Whitehead's paper reviews the disposition of WWII aircraft remains donated from Japan to the Naval History and Heritage Command. Khakzad presents research on stone anchors found along the northern shoreline of the Persian Gulf. Finally, Fleming and Haines review their efforts to better address storage, conservation, and collections needs at the Mariner's Museum and Park.

As has been the case with this recent run of the Proceedings, which began in 2007, this publication would not be possible without the gracious assistance and oversight of the PAST Foundation, and in particular Dr. Sheli Smith.

DAVID BALL
CHRISTOPHER HORRELL

The Fate of *Far West*:

Geophyiscal Investigations to Locate the Wreck of an Iconic Upper Missouri River Mountain Packet Steamboat

Douglas D. Scott, Bert Ho, Sadie Dasovich, Steve Dasovich, and David L. Conlin

Far West is legendary as part of the history of steamboating on the Upper Missouri River. It is noteworthy for its association with the 1876 Battle of the Little Bighorn. It represents the whole class of mountain packets that plied the Missouri River in the 1870s. Far West's service ended as a lower Missouri River steamboat engaged in local trade until she snagged on October 20, 1883 and sank. Side scanning sonar and magnetometer data were collected in the Missouri River channel near the likely wreck site. Two anomalies may be associated with known historic steamboat landings or a steamboat wreck.

Introduction

Far West is legendary as part of the history of steamboating on the Upper Missouri River. It is especially noteworthy for its association with the 1876 Battle of the Little Bighorn. In many ways *Far West* is iconic as an historically well documented steamboat employed in the Missouri River trade and transport (Figure 1). It is representative of the whole class of mountain packets that plied the Missouri River in the 1870s.

FIGURE 1: *Far West* Patrolling the Tongue River, 1878. From *Frank Leslie's Illustrated Newspaper*, July 27, 1878.

Like many of her class, *Far West* came to an ignominious end. She outlived her usefulness as an Upper Missouri packet, was sold off by her original owners, and ended her service as a lower Missouri River steamboat engaged in local trade. She transported household and agricultural goods up and down the lower Missouri River until she snagged on October 20, 1883 and sank in five feet of water. The cargo, engines, boilers, and most of the superstructure down to the waterline were salvaged within a few days, leaving her lower hull as the only physical reminder of this once famous and proud steamboat.

Missouri's ties to water-related resources and water transportation are woefully underrepresented in public history venues and resources. Missouri exists the way it does today, mostly because of the Mississippi and Missouri Rivers. The submerged cultural resources of the state have received little attention and are often damaged or destroyed due to various projects. This is largely due to the mistaken impression that those resources have been destroyed or so damaged from being underwater that they have no historical value left. Underwater archaeologists know this is often not true (Petsche 1974; Corbin 2000; 2006a; Kane 2004; Lopinot and Thompson 2013). Underwater environments often act to preserve organic materials and shipwrecks are prime examples of this scenario.

Lindenwood University's Department of Anthropology and Archaeological Research Program received a grant from the Missouri Humanities Council (2085) to conduct an archaeological survey for the wreck site of *Far West*. The grant allowed Lindenwood to assemble a team of archaeologists to document and search for the remains of *Far West* using the latest underwater archaeology methods. The National Park Service's Submerged Resources Center (SRC) provided qualified marine archaeologists and remote sensing geophysical equipment to conduct a systematic search for the wreck site.

Brief History of *Far West*

Construction and Specifications

Far West was built in Pittsburgh in 1870 for the Coulson Packet Company at a cost of $24,000. *Far West* was 188 feet (58 m) long with a beam of 33 feet (10 m) and had three decks, a cupola-like pilot house and two tall smoke stacks. She drew only 20 inches (51 cm) of water unloaded and 30 inches (76 cm) loaded with 186 tons of freight. Between her first and second decks were two powerful high pressure steam engines built by Herbertson Engine Works of Brownsville, Pennsylvania, each with 15 inch (38 cm) diameter pistons and a 5 foot (1.5 m) stroke. The engines were powered by steam from three boilers that consumed as many as 30 cords of wood a day. The engines drove a single 30 foot (9.1 m) wide stern wheel. *Far West* also had two steam capstans, one on each side of the bow, reportedly the first boat built with more than one. The cargo capacity fully loaded was 397.8 tons (Annual Report of the Quartermaster General 1876).

Far West was built for the Coulson company as an Upper Missouri River packet boat. Generally, *Far West* and its sister boats sailed between Sioux City or Yankton, South Dakota (then Dakota Territory) up river to the head of navigation, Fort Benton, Montana. The company regularly contracted with the Department of the Interior to deliver Indian annuities to various agents for distribution to the tribes required under various treaty obligations. Likewise, the company also contracted with the U. S. Army for transport of men and supplies to the various up river forts and camps, as well as transporting supplies for various expeditions (Lass 1962; 1985; 2008; Scott et al. 2018).

Far West is first reported as an active steamer on the Upper Missouri River on October 19, 1870 (The Yankton Press) just months after it was built and fitted out. Newspapers along the Upper Missouri reported steamboat departures and arrivals, as well as some delays due to river conditions and accidents (Lepley 2001).

Far West was a well-known boat on the Upper Missouri prior to 1876, but it was its performance in transporting the Little Bighorn battle wounded to Fort Abraham Lincoln in record time that made it truly famous (Gray 1968). The steamboat did not just happen to be in the area, it was contracted along with other Coulson line boats to transport men and material during the campaign seasons of 1876 and 1877.

The story of Captain Grant Marsh's epic dash from the juncture of the Little Bighorn and Big Horn Rivers to Fort Lincoln with battle wounded, in record time, is literally the stuff of legend (Chittenden 1962:387-390; Hanson 2003). Although not neglected in history, but often little mentioned in the Little Bighorn literature, is the movement of the wounded from the valley camp to the meeting with the steamboat *Far West* (Scott et al. 2018)

Far West, like many other steamboats on the Upper Missouri, plied the waters carrying commercial goods for the next several years. The Coulson Packet line sold *Far West* to Durfee and Peck of the Northwest Transportation Company in 1880. The steamboat continued service on the Upper Missouri until 1882 when it was sold to H. N. Dodd and Victor Bonnett. *Far West* entered the lower Missouri short trade route in November 1882 (St. Louis Globe-Democrat 1882).

In just over eleven months, until its snagging and sinking on October 20, 1883, *Far West* made routine runs up and down the lower Missouri River from St. Louis to Tuscumbia and return. Its trips up and down the river were regularly reported by the St. Louis Globe-Democrat in its Rivers column. The normal cargo for the now 13-year-old steamboat were hardware and goods from St. Louis meant for the upriver communities. The downstream cargo consisted largely of farm produce meant for the St. Louis market (Scott et al. 2018)

On the morning of October 20, the aged steamboat struck a snag near the head of Mullanphy Island, below St. Charles as reported in a German language newspaper (St. Charles Demokrat 1883). She settled in five feet of water with a reported four inches of water on her starboard side with her larboard side dry (St. Louis Anzeiger Des Westens Sonntagsblatt 1883). The St. Louis Globe-Democrat (1883a) reported *Far West* was valued at $8000.00, but there was no insurance on the boat (Figure 2). This value was one-third of her original construction price. However, the cargo was fully insured and consisted of 3,000 sacks of grain, 135 barrels of apples, 11,000 packages of sundries and bulk meats, and 73 head of hogs. Most of the cargo was saved. The wreck was salvaged and its decking, pilot house, boilers, cylinders, steam pipes, other machinery, and even its kitchen stove, cooking utensils, and other miscellaneous items were sold at public auction (Figure 3) on October 31, 1883 at St. Louis (St. Louis Globe-Democrat 1883b).

All that likely remained of the once proud and famous steamboat was its snag-damaged and broken lower hull, some of its internal trussing or hog chain system, and perhaps some of its paddle wheel. Over the years the ever-changing Missouri River enveloped the wreck, hiding it from view.

The Likely Wreck Site Area

Wrecks occurred from the time steamboats began plying the Missouri River. It is estimated that between 600 and 800 steamboats wrecked on the Missouri River system between 1819 and 1941. Some of those were saved and returned to operation, but most were lost,

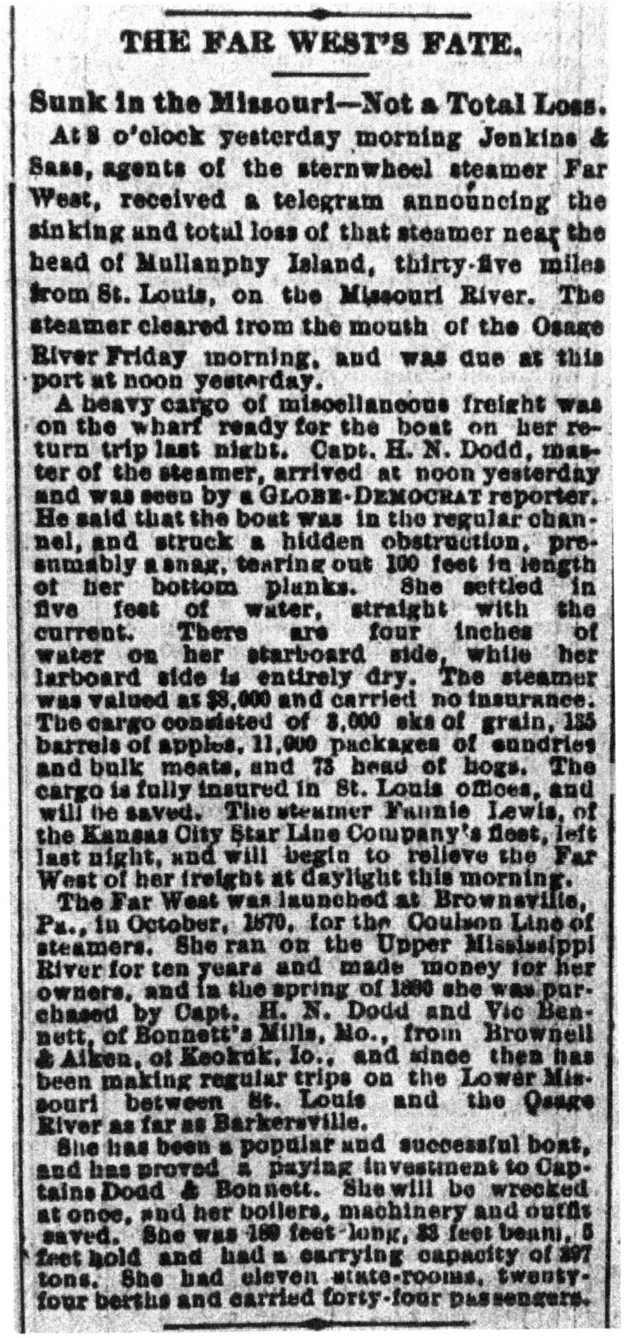

THE FAR WEST'S FATE.

Sunk in the Missouri—Not a Total Loss.

At 8 o'clock yesterday morning Jenkins & Sass, agents of the sternwheel steamer Far West, received a telegram announcing the sinking and total loss of that steamer near the head of Mullanphy Island, thirty-five miles from St. Louis, on the Missouri River. The steamer cleared from the mouth of the Osage River Friday morning, and was due at this port at noon yesterday.

A heavy cargo of miscellaneous freight was on the wharf ready for the boat on her return trip last night. Capt. H. N. Dodd, master of the steamer, arrived at noon yesterday and was seen by a GLOBE-DEMOCRAT reporter. He said that the boat was in the regular channel, and struck a hidden obstruction, presumably a snag, tearing out 100 feet in length of her bottom planks. She settled in five feet of water, straight with the current. There are four inches of water on her starboard side, while her larboard side is entirely dry. The steamer was valued at $8,000 and carried no insurance. The cargo consisted of 8,000 sks of grain, 135 barrels of apples, 11,000 packages of sundries and bulk meats, and 73 head of hogs. The cargo is fully insured in St. Louis offices, and will be saved. The steamer Fannie Lewis, of the Kansas City Star Line Company's fleet, left last night, and will begin to relieve the Far West of her freight at daylight this morning.

The Far West was launched at Brownsville, Pa., in October, 1870, for the Coulson Line of steamers. She ran on the Upper Mississippi River for ten years and made money for her owners, and in the spring of 1880 she was purchased by Capt. H. N. Dodd and Vic Bennett, of Bonnett's Mills, Mo., from Brownell & Aiken, of Keokuk, Io., and since then has been making regular trips on the Lower Missouri between St. Louis and the Osage River as far as Barkersville.

She has been a popular and successful boat, and has proved a paying investment to Captains Dodd & Bonnett. She will be wrecked at once, and her boilers, machinery and outfit saved. She was 189 feet long, 33 feet beam, 5 feet hold and had a carrying capacity of 397 tons. She had eleven state-rooms, twenty-four berths and carried forty-four passengers.

FIGURE 2: *St. Louis Globe-Democrat* article (October 21, 1883) detailing the wreck of *Far West.*

many to snagging. Capt. Hiram Chittenden, an Army engineer, with significant Missouri River experience was assigned to the Missouri River Commission in 1884. Among his duties was assembling a list and map of steamboat wrecks on the Missouri and its tributaries (Chittenden 1970). The list and map were produced in 1897. Among the hundreds of wrecks located on the map is the approximate site of *Far West* wreck.

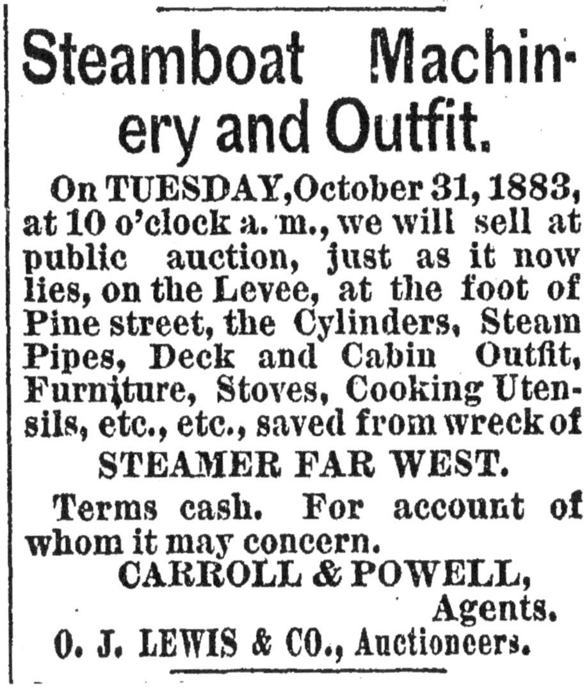

Steamboat Machinery and Outfit.

On TUESDAY, October 31, 1883, at 10 o'clock a. m., we will sell at public auction, just as it now lies, on the Levee, at the foot of Pine street, the Cylinders, Steam Pipes, Deck and Cabin Outfit, Furniture, Stoves, Cooking Utensils, etc., etc., saved from wreck of STEAMER FAR WEST.

Terms cash. For account of whom it may concern.

CARROLL & POWELL, Agents.

O. J. LEWIS & CO., Auctioneers.

FIGURE 3: Advertisement for the sale of salvaged fittings from *Far West* in the *St. Louis Globe-Democrat,* October 28, 1883.

In partnership with Lindenwood University, the SRC provided boat support and two archeologists for a remote sensing survey in the Missouri River for the steamboat *Far West.* Survey areas based on archival research and historic maps of the river were created for the project, and the SRC conducted both a side scan sonar survey and a marine magnetometer survey of those areas.

2017 Side Scan Sonar Survey

On September 15th and 16th, SRC vessel *Cal Cummings* was launched from St. Charles, Missouri and transited down river approximately five miles to the survey area. A Klein 3000H high definition, dual frequency (455 kHz and 900 kHz) side scan sonar was used for the entirety of the survey. Due to the shallow depths within the survey block, a side tow method was used to keep the sonar tow fish close to the surface along the port side of SRC's vessel, *Cal Cummings.*

For the survey area near *Far West* both high (900kHz) and low (455kHz) frequencies were used at a range of 50 meters. At the request of Lindenwood University, sonar surveys were also conducted at the wreck site of steamboat Montana. This site was extensively mapped by archeologists (Corbin 2006b; Corbin and Rodgers 2008) and collecting sonar surveys over the area provides a glimpse of the sediment coverage over the wreck. It also serves as an assessment of the deeper portions of the site to identify any areas that may be eroding or collapsing further into the river channel. Another unidentified steamboat wreck was surveyed just upriver of the boat ramp on the St. Charles side.

All sonar data was post-processed with Chesapeake Technology's SonarWiz 7.0, and exported as GeoTIFFs. Portions of the primary survey area were too shallow for *Cal Cummings* to safely navigate, and surveys with a shallow draft vessel were necessary to complete all historically suspected areas for the remains of this vessel.

Magnetometer Survey

Once the sonar surveys were complete, the magnetometer survey in the same areas was done. SRC provided a Geometrics 882 marine magnetometer equipped with both an altimeter and a depth sensor. It was rigged for a nose tow, and to keep it close to the surface in the shallow river, several bullet floats were added to the cable and tow fish.

Approximately 10 linear nautical miles of magnetometer surveys were conducted in the survey block for *Far West*, and along both shores of the river upstream and downstream of that area. Due to time constraints, multiple parallel lines were not run in the center of the river, and the shallowness of the *Far West* survey area also prevented additional survey lines inshore. A shallow draft vessel was required for a future survey of the area.

All magnetometer data was post processed in Hypack 2016, and anomalies were also selected in the Hypack single beam processor. Those anomalies were then exported as a text file and converted into an Excel spreadsheet as XYZ data. A total of 95 anomalies were detected just for the survey lines in and around *Far West* survey block. Additional magnetometer surveys were conducted around the wreck of Montana and the unidentified steamboat upriver of the boat ramp in St. Charles. Those data were collected to provide a comparative sample of what a steamboat signature, minus boilers, and engines, would appear as in the gamma readings within the Missouri River.

2018 Magnetometer Survey

With higher water levels the team returned to the Missouri River in June 2018 to conduct a magnetometer survey to locate *Far West* in an area of the river between some older rock wing dams that correlated well with historic maps of where *Far West* was wrecked. For this survey, SRC's Geometric G-882 marine magnetometer at two hertz was used to survey a stretch of river approximately one-third of a mile long, collecting 1.6 linear nautical miles of magnetometer data. This area was smaller than the side scan survey area, but it was much closer to shore and much more focused at the suspected wreck location.

There are three anomalies interpreted as having the highest potential to be cultural material, not related to the wing dams. These anomalies are far enough away from the wing dams to not be associated with them, they have strong gamma readings (approximately 105 gammas for the highest), and they are not in areas of known cables or remnants of cables. These are located in shallow water about 15 meters from the current shoreline. Additional dense magnetometer surveys of these anomalies and the areas around them will delineate the extents of the possible site. This could also be done with divers using hand held metal detectors, and hand probes to locate buried material. If these anomalies are indeed related to *Far West*, we suspect more anomalies will be found with a denser magnetometer survey. It appears likely portions of the wreck are buried on shore and in the river bank (Figure 4).

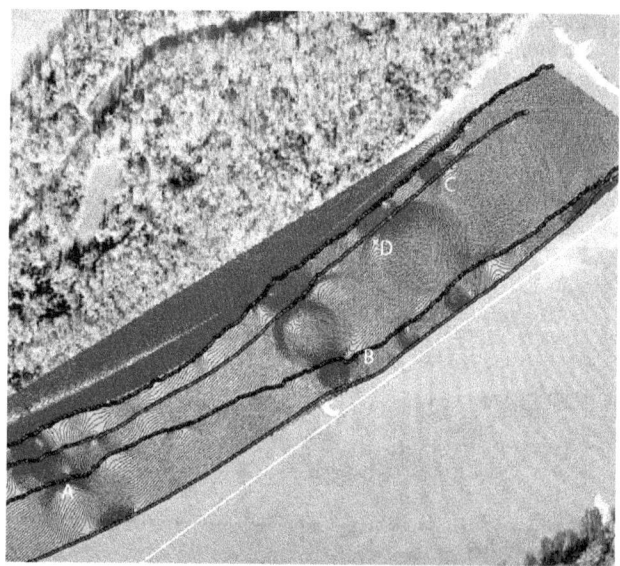

FIGURE 4: A detailed view of the 2018 magnetic anomalies from left to right two wing dams (A and B) and two unknown anomalies (C, D). The anomaly (C) may be a steamboat landing as the location is consistent with that location on the Chittenden map. Anomaly D is unknown but is consistent with a steamboat wreck.

Results and Conclusions

Based on the analysis of both the 2017 sonar and magnetometer data and additional survey operations with a magnetometer in 2018 with a shallow draft vessel, a number of large magnetic anomalies were identified in the location of the historically documented wreck site. Two are associated with river control features known as wing dams. Three require additional investigation to determine their origin and function. One or more may represent the remains of local landowners' steamboat landings, and one corresponds to an oval-shaped wooden feature that is seen on the 1996 low water imagery. The data do not conclusively identify a steamboat wreck, but the features are consistent and deserve more detailed examination to confirm their origin and function.

The Missouri River is very dynamic with changing eddies and currents creating islands that move seasonally if not weekly. This constant movement will undoubtedly carry ferrous material and redeposit it down river, and it also may carry away shipwrecks and all associated artifacts. When looking at the magnetic anomalies visually, it is both encouraging and slightly overwhelming. It is clear there are significant ferrous materials near the survey area for *Far West*, but it is also evident that there are anomalies along the entire length of the survey lines and likely the whole river. What can be concluded is that we have a better understanding of how best to move forward with survey operations in the future in this part of the Missouri River.

Acknowledgements

We express our gratitude and appreciation to Steven Belko and the Missouri Humanities Council for their support and guidance. Greg Wolk was also generous with his advice and support during the project. We sincerely appreciate the advice and ideas of Dr. Annalies Corbin during the early development stage of the project. Our thanks and appreciation are extended to Lindenwood University anthropology students Collin Rossen and Amanda Erdei who volunteered for the initial search efforts on the Missouri River. Likewise we thank Lindenwood University administrative personnel for their hard work to make the logistics happen. We also thank Murphy Library, Special Collections staff, University of Wisconsin-La Crosse and the staff of the Missouri History Museum Archives for their assistance in locating photographs and documents relating to the history of *Far West*.

References

Anzeiger Des Westens Sonntagsblatt
1883   Der Dampfer "*Far West*" descheitert. *Anzeiger Des Westens Sonntagsblatt*, October 21, 1883.

Chittenden, Hiram Martin
1962   History of Early Steamboat Navigation on the Missouri River: Life and Adventures of Joseph La Barge. Ross and Haines, Minneapolis, Minn.

1970   Report of Steamboat Wrecks on the Missouri River. *Nebraska History* 51:16-23.

Corbin, Annalies
2000   *The Material Culture of Steamboat Passengers: Archaeological Evidence from the Missouri River.* Kluwer Academic Press, New York.

2006a   *The Life and Times of the Steamboat Red Cloud.* Texas A&M University Press, College Station.

2006b   Steamboat *Montana* (1879-1884) – Leviathan of the American Plains. The International Journal of Nautical Archaeology 36(1):59-74

Corbin, Annalies and Bradley A. Rodgers
2008   *The Steamboat Montana and the Opening of the West: History, Excavation, and Architecture.* University Press of Florida, Gainesville.

Gray, John S.
1968   Medical Service on the Little Big Horn Campaign. *Westerners Brand Book* 24(11):81-83, 86-88.

Hanson, Joseph Mills
2003   *The Conquest of the Missouri.* Stackpole, Mechanicsburg, Penn. Reprint of 1909 edition.

Kane, Adam I.
2004   *The Western River Steamboat.* Texas A&M Press, College Station.

Lass, William E.
1962   *A History of Steamboating on the Upper Missouri River.* University of Nebraska Press, Lincoln.

1985   Steamboats on the Yellowstone. *Montana*, The Magazine of Western History 35(4):26-41.

2008   *Navigating the Missouri: Steamboating on Nature's Highway, 1819-1935.* The Arthur H. Clark Company, Norman, Okla.

Lepley, John G.
2001   *Packets to Paradise: Steamboating to Fort Benton.* Pictorial Histories Publishing, Missoula, Mont.

LOPINOT, NEAL H. AND DUSTIN A. THOMPSON
2013 A Shipwreck Magnetometer Survey on Jameson Island, Saline County, and Cora Island, St. Charles County, Missouri. Center for Archaeological Research, Research Report 1469, Missouri State University, Springfield.

PETSCHE, JEROME E.
1974 *The Steamboat Bertrand: History, Excavation, and Architecture.* National Park Service, Government Printing Office, Washington, DC.

SCOTT, DOUGLAS, BERT HO, SADIE DASOVICH, STEVE DASOVICH, AND DAVID CONLIN
2018 The Fate of *Far West:* Historic Documentation and the 2017 and 2018 Remote Sensing Searches for the Wreck Site. Prepared for Missouri Humanities Council Grant 2085, Department of Anthropology, Lindenwood University, St. Charles, MO.

ST. CHARLES DEMOKRAT
1883 Aus Missouri. *St. Charles Demokrat*, October 25, 1883.

ST. LOUIS GLOBE DEMOCRAT
1882 Rivers Column, The *Far West* has entered the short trade in Missouri. *St. Louis Globe Democrat*, November 12, 1882.

1883a *The* Far West's *Fate. St. Louis Globe Democrat,* October 21, 1883.

1883b Advertisement, Steamboat Machinery and Outfit. *St. Louis Globe Democrat*, October 28, 1883.

WAR DEPARTMENT
1876 *Annual Report of the Quartermaster General to the Secretary of War.* Government Printing Office, Washington D.C.

. . . .

Douglas D. Scott,
2219 Renaissance Blvd, Grand Junction, CO 81507
Cell – 402-429-3268
Dougdscott1@gmail.com
Primary contact for all edits, etc.

Bert Ho,
Project Manager, Regulatory, Archeologist
U.S. Army Corps of Engineers South Pacific Division
Phillip Burton Federal Building
P.O. Box 36023
450 Golden Gate Ave.
San Francisco, CA 94102
Office 415-503-6778
Bert.ho@gmail.com

Sadie Dasovich,
Department of History and Anthropology
Howard Hall, Room 350
Monmouth University
400 Cedar Ave.
West Long Branch, NU 07764
ssdasovich@sbcglobal.net

Steve Dasovich
Anthropology and Sociology Department
Young Hall 108B
Lindenwood University
St. Charles, MO 63301
Cell 314-609-6132
Office 636-255-2223
sdasovich@lindenwood.edu

David Conlin
David L. Conlin Ph.D.
Archeologist, Chief
National Park Service
Submerged Resources Center
12795 West Alameda Pkwy.
Lakewood, CO 80228
(303) 969-2665
Dave_Conlin@nps.gov

Coming in with a Tide, Going out with a Forklift: The Spring Break Shipwreck Project

Allyson Ropp

The Spring Break wreckage washed ashore in St. Augustine in March 2018. It created a cultural phenomenon with stories and images spreading worldwide. The project brought out thousands of people and a drive to document as much as possible before the coming tide, using traditional and digital recording. The race against the tide pushed the decision to move the wreck remains to the Guana Tolomato Matanzas National Estuarine Research Reserve. This paper will provide an overview of the fieldwork and public interpretation of the hull feature while on the beach, its transportation from the beach, and current outreach efforts.

Introduction

In late March 2018, an unexpected surprise arrived on the beachfront doorstep of a family vacationing along Ponte Vedra Beach. Little did they know, while they slept that night, a 50 foot section of a wooden vessel would wash ashore to surprise them the next morning. As a mother and son wandered the beach that morning, they encountered this large section of hull remains. And thus began a new adventure for that shipwreck. Almost immediately various local organizations arrived to ensure no one passing would cut the remains to bits, media stormed the beach to share the exciting discovery with the local community, and archaeologists assembled to document the remains before they washed away again.

The wreckage stayed on the beach that night. The archaeological team and thousands of visitors returned to the beach over the following days to record the feature and to witness the awe-inspiring nature of the vessel debris. Given the name Spring Break Wreck, because of the timing of the find, the remains became a cultural phenomenon. The hull feature was recorded using traditional mapping methods as well as digital means to create three-dimensional models. As more people saw the wreck for themselves and noticed it slowly degrading along the beach, the public pushed for its further protection. Efforts were made to move the remains out of the high tide zone, before its final move off the beach. The wreckage has now become an educational tool in the Guana Tolomato Matanzas National Estuarine Research Reserve (GTM-NERR), and it continues to inspire young and old alike to learn about the mysteries of the sea. This paper outlines the events of the archaeological work conducted on the remains, discusses the cooperative effort to preserve and protect the feature, and summarizes the educational uses of this artifact in its current home.

Site Background

The wooden hull remains of the Spring Break Wreck washed ashore from the Atlantic Ocean along the Ponte Vedra Beach coastline. It was discovered approximately one mile north of the GTM-NERR educational center. The beach is a part of the GTM-NERR, which consists of 73,352 acres spanning nearly 40 miles of coastal lands in St. Johns and Flagler counties along the northeast coast of Florida (Florida Department of Environmental Protection 2018). Offshore of the beach, the environment consists of shoals and bars subject to strong currents, tidal fluctuations, and seasonal storms.

Discovery and Project Timeline

The hull feature was first discovered by a vacationing family walking down the beach in late March 2018. Upon discovery, the family altered local authorities of its presence. The St. Johns County Sheriff's Office, Florida Fish and Wildlife, and GTM-NERR staff all proceeded to the beach to ensure the wreckage was not disturbed. Simultaneously, the media learned of the presence of the remains. By noon on 28 March, news outlets from St. Augustine and Jacksonville made their way to the beach to report on the discovery of the wreck debris. News outlets reported on the wreck with titles such as "Shipwreck in Ponte Vedra may be from 18th century," "'Old' shipwreck washes ashore in Ponte Vedra Beach," and "A shipwreck, possibly from the 18th century, found washed ashore Florida Beach" (Micolucci 2018; Scanlan 2018; Putterman 2018). The news sent imaginations flying about the history of the hull remains, its age, and its previous location.

As the news was spreading, the St. Augustine Lighthouse Archaeological Maritime Program (LAMP) headed to the location to jump in front of the media before more sensationalized stories could spread. The team, upon arrival, conducted a preliminary assessment of the site while concurrently dealing with the various news outlets present on the beach (Figure 1). Unsure of whether the wreckage would be there the coming day, the team gathered as much information as possible during that first day. Preliminary sketches and measurements were made of the entirety of the wreck remains including the overall length and beam. Photographs were taken of the entirety of the wreck debris, including interesting features, such as treenails and marks along the frames. Additionally, a photogrammetric model was made to preserve the initial form. After collecting this information and sharing initial discoveries with the press, the team left unsure of whether it would still be there the next morning.

The next morning, the discovering family alerted the team that it was still on the beach. Archaeologists returned to the site to conduct further documentation and to develop a strategy to protect the wreckage from harm, both environmental and human. The main archaeological focus of the day centered on noting and documenting the changes between Day 1 and Day 2, which included a significant loss of timbers on the ocean side (Figure 2). As the team now knew it was unlikely this feature would wash back to sea as a unit, and with increased interest of the local community, the team had to devise a way to protect the remains. An effort was made to move the hull remains out of high tidal zone, but a forklift acquired for the job sank immediately into the beach. The wreckage was temporarily lashed to the beach to ensure it would be present in the following days before a solid plan could be implemented to move it.

The next two days were spent recording the hull remains. Wood samples and biological samples were taken for further analysis (see Burke, this publication). The media and public remained present on the beach for the entirety of the first week, as news continued to spread around the country and the world (Figure 3). News headlines exploded with titles such as "Florida beachgoers discover 'holy grail of shipwrecks' after remains of 18th century ship wash ashore," "Preservationists race to save old shipwreck battered by waves on Florida beach," and "Centuries-old shipwreck washes up in Florida" (Farber 2018; CBS Interactive 2018; Daley 2018). With the stories developing and intrigue growing, archaeologists also had the responsibility of sharing their preliminary findings with the public.

FIGURE 1: LAMP archaeologists discussing with the media the new find and taking initial overall measurements of the site (Photo by LAMP 2018).

FIGURE 2: Side by side comparison of the Spring Break Wreck between Day 1 (left) and Day 2 (right). Notice there is a change between the two days. More wreckage is present on Day 1 as compared to Day 2 (Photos by LAMP and FPAN 2018).

FIGURE 3: LAMP archaeologists and volunteers mapping the remains of the Spring Break Wreck with a multitude of visitors gathered around watching the process and learning about the wreck (Photo by LAMP 2018).

Approximately one month later, after recovery plans had been developed, on 19 April 2018 the wreckage was removed from the beach. With the assistance of local community member John Valdes, and support from the State of Florida and other community officials, a team from Construction Debris Removal lifted the hull remains and drove it down the beach using a John Deere 544K wheel loader. The remains were placed on a flat-bed truck to transfer to the GTM-NERR trailhead. There the loader placed it in its final location. Today, the wreckage sits at the front of the trailhead with signage discussing its construction and historical significance (Figure 4).

Archaeological Methodology

The hull feature was recorded and analyzed using a variety of different archaeological methods. Traditional methods of recording were used to document the entirety of the remains over the first three days of the project. The feature was mapped to scale in a plan view using tape measures and rulers. Additional information was gathered including frame spacing and thickness to understand the construction of the wrecked vessel.

Digital recording occurred continuously throughout the project, and still continues with site visits as they happen. Photographs of the overall site and intricate details were taken every day of the project. Additional sets of photographs were taken to create numerous photogrammetric models of the feature. The photos were processed and modeled using *Agisoft Photoscan*. The photos and photogrammetric models were used to not only document each day of work, but also to show and monitor the changes to the wreckage across time. The University of South Florida (USF) participated in this project to conduct laser scanning of the hull feature. The USF team from the Digital Heritage and Humanities Collection conducted the scan and created a scaled and geo-rectified 3-dimensional model.

Selective sampling was done as well to conduct further tests in the lab. First, wood samples were collected from twenty-three locations across the hull remains. The samples were primarily taken to determine the different wood species represented. The wood samples were transported to Dr. Lee Newsom at Flagler College for analysis. The second set of samples gathered was of biological marine growth. These samples were taken by Jessica Whelpley, a graduate student at the University of Florida working with the Whitney Marine Lab in St. Augustine, Florida.

Site Results and Analysis

On the day of discovery, the site measured 14.58 m (47.83 ft.) in overall length. It consisted of thirteen

FIGURE 4: The Construction Debris Removal team moving the wreck down the beach (left), placing the remains at the trailhead in the GTM-NERR (middle), and the wreck structure in its final home at the trailhead (right) (Photos by LAMP 2018).

outer hull planks, thirteen frame sets, and seven ceiling planks. Visible across all the timbers were treenail holes with treenails still present as well as some iron fasteners and iron concretion. Observed on the outer side of the outer hull planks were tacks, indicating this wrecked vessel was sheathed. A large hooked scarf joint is present in one of the ceiling planks. Tool marks from various tools and saws were clearly seen in the wood. Roman numerals were also observed etched into each frame pair. Additionally, an arrow was etched into one of the frames pointing towards the outer hull planking beneath.

Day two showed some change in the structure (Figure 2). The wreckage had lost three outer hull planks, the most exposed row of futtocks from the frames, and three ceiling planks. These timbers were stripped from the hull remains by the rising and falling of the tides and the pounding of the waves overnight. The wreckage was almost three feet shorter than the previous day because of the missing timbers. The lost futtocks did reveal that each futtock in a frame pair was labeled with corresponding roman numerals on the interior faces of each futtock. These were numbered 18 (XVIII) through 31(XXXI) (see Meide this publication for construction analysis).

The wood samples collected revealed the wrecked vessel was constructed of three different types of tree. The frames were Southern Yellow Pine (*Pinus taeda*) and American Beech (*Fagus grandifolia*). The planks and treenails were white oak (*Quercus alba*) (Lee Newsom 2018, pers. comm.; see Burke and Newsome this publication for further analysis). At the time of this writing, the results of the biological analysis are being processed and analyzed.

Protection and Monitoring

As the media interest in the hull feature grew and it did not wash away, the team became concerned in the preservation of the wreckage. The team consisted of more than the LAMP archaeologists working on the remains. The GTM-NERR monitors the beach on which the wreckage washed ashore and became the immediate protectors. Most importantly as the hull section had washed ashore in Florida, the remains belong to the state of Florida, meaning the Division of Historical Resources and the State Historic Preservation Officer had the final say in the future of the artifact. They were concerned not only about the beating the wreckage was taking from the waves and tides, but also the human element of salvage and physically pulling the remains apart. With these threats in mind and the large push from the community to save the wreckage, all options were discussed. These options were to (a) leave the hull remains on the beach and let the seas take it back; (b) recover the remains from the tidal zone and leave it on the beach; and (c) remove it from the beach and relocate it to a new home at the GTM-NERR. Community pressure and consideration led to the third option (c) to be selected for the wreckage. The option of conservation was briefly considered, but space and financial prospects were unavailable for such an option to be selected.

In order to move the hull feature from the beach, heavy equipment was needed. The hull remains were located almost a mile from the nearest public access area and weighed almost 5,000 pounds. As mentioned previously, on the second day of the project an attempt was made to move the wreckage from the tidal zone. However, the equipment was not sufficient enough to travel down the beach. Working with community partners, the Construction Debris Removal team was able to get a large front loader on to the beach and transport it to the GTM-NERR.

The wreckage is now protected from both people and the tidal environment. It sits behind a wooden barrier to help deter people from taking wood off the wreckage. Issues now facing the hull remains include continuous sun exposure and wood eating organisms. The GTM-NERR is currently spraying the ground around the hull remains with a pesticide to keep most of the insects from causing further damage. The sun exposure is much more difficult to deal with. As there is no funding for this project, a cover has not yet been built to shield it from the sun. The sun is continuously drying the wood out, causing the wood to shrink and splinter as its cells lose their support. This process will continue to happen until the wood completely deteriorates.

Education and Outreach

The magic of this artifact is not in its historical significance, but in the tools it can provide for public education about maritime archaeology. As the wreckage attracted thousands of visitors over the course of a few days, it was meticulously documented and studied by archaeologists. Visitors were exposed not only to the immediate discovery of the hull remains, but also to all sorts of aspects of cultural heritage management and archaeological and conservation processes rarely discussed with the general populace (Figure 3). Each day one of the archaeologists was tasked with answering questions about the hull remains as well the jobs the other archaeologists were conducting. This included discussion of archaeological recording methods, sampling methods, and artifact deterioration.

With the wreckage in an accessible location, it still acts as a training tool. LAMP has already taken groups of students to the site to discuss ship construction. The hull remains are suitable to practicing scaled mapping of shipwreck sites without the restrictions imposed by conducting these training sessions in water. For the general public, the wreckage is still accessible and signage is in place. This signage discusses the archaeological information of the hull remains as well as conservation principles, including why it is drying out.

The hull remains also allow for a deeper discussion of the protection of cultural heritage and climate change. The wreckage appeared more than likely because of storms in the area. The surge on the bottom had moved enough sand to shift the remains from the seafloor to the beach. As the overall environment changes and storms become more frequent, there is a potential for more incidents like the Spring Break Wreck to occur. This opens the floor for discussion on how to protect such artifacts that wash ashore and brings up important questions for managers and the general public to consider for future protection of submerged cultural remains and the changing environmental landscape.

Conclusions

As the wreckage was something that appeared on the beach, it became a cultural phenomenon. Through media reports, its appearance spread across the country. In the immediate area, the wreckage brought thousands of people to the beach to see it and archaeologists in action to save the hull remains. While the hull remains are not those of a 16th century galleon or 18th century pirate ship as many visitors and media outlets suggested, it provides an opportunity to educate and inspire nonetheless. A mere 19th century merchant vessel, the hull remains show a world of decay and preservation. It provides an opportunity to teach about archaeological resources, preservation of cultural remains through recordation and study, protection by the public to ensure others can enjoy learning the same, and imagination to continue to explore those lost at sea.

Acknowledgements

The author and LAMP would like to thank the GTM-NERR, the Florida Bureau of Archaeological Research, the Florida Public Archaeology Network, USF Digital Heritage and Humanities Collection, UF Whitney Marine Lab, Dr. Lee Newsom of Flagler College, SEARCH Inc., John Valdes, Construction Debris Removal, Sunbelt Rentals, the guests and residents of Florida A1A along Ponte Vedra Beach, and the local community for supporting this archaeological research and aiding the preservation of an amazing discovery.

References

CBS INTERACTIVE
2018 Preservationists race to save old shipwreck battered by waves on Florida beach. CBS/AP. <https://www.cbsnews.com/news/florida-shipwreck-preservationists-south-ponte-vedra-beach/>. Accessed 04 Dec 2018.

DALEY, JASON
2018 Centuries-old shipwreck washes up in Florida. Smithsonian.com. <https://www.smithsonianmag.com/smart-news/200-year-old-shipwreck-washes-florida-180968629/>. Accessed 04 Dec 2018.

FARBER, MADELINE
2018 Florida beachgoers discover 'holy grail of shipwrecks' after remains of 18th century ship wash ashore. Fox News. <https://www.foxnews.com/science/florida-beachgoers-discover-holy-grail-of-shipwrecks-after-remains-of-18th-century-ship-wash-ashore>. Accessed 04 Dec 2018.

Florida Department of Environmental Protection
2018 National Estuarine Research Reserves-Guana-Tolomato-Matanzas. Florida Department of Environmental Protection. <https://floridadep.gov/fco/nerr-gtm>. Accessed 04 Dec 2018.

MICOLUCCI, VIC
2018 Shipwreck in Ponte Vedra may be from 18th century. News4JAX. <https://www.news4jax.com/news/florida/st-johns-county/part-of-ships-hull-washes-ashore-in-ponte-vedra>. Accessed 04 Dec 2018.

PUTTERMAN, SAMANTHA
2018 A shipwreck, possibly form the 18th century, found washed ashore Florida beach. *Bradenton Herald*. <https://www.bradenton.com/news/local/article207228794.html>. Accessed 04 Dec 2018.

SCANLAN, DAN
2018 'Old' shipwreck washes ashore in Ponte Vedra Beach. *The Florida Times-Union*. <https://www.firstcoastnews.com/article/news/local/old-shipwreck-washes-ashore-in-ponte-vedra-beach/77-532964773>. Accessed 04 Dec 2018.

· · · · · · · · · · · · · · · ·

Allyson Ropp
St. Augustine Lighthouse & Maritime Museum
81 Lighthouse Ave
St. Augustine, FL 32080
904-829-0745
aropp@staugustinelighthouse.org

Hull Remains of the Spring Break Wreck, a Nineteenth-Century Shipwreck Washed Ashore at Ponte Vedra Beach, Florida

Chuck Meide

On 28 March 2018, after several days of foul weather, a large section of articulated hull remains unexpectedly washed ashore at Ponte Vedra Beach in northeast Florida. Around 15 meters in length, the timbers represented a substantial section of a large ocean-going vessel. When first encountered, the timbers were in excellent condition, with tool marks and shipwright scribing clearly visible to researchers. A number of idiosyncrasies were noted, including Roman numerals on frames, spacers to separate paired futtocks, and square pegs forced through round holes to transversely fasten them. Analysis suggests this craft was built in a vernacular yard in the southeastern U.S. sometime around the 1880s-1890s.

Introduction

In the morning hours of 28 March 2018, beachgoers at South Ponte Vedra Beach, in North Florida between the Jacksonville Beaches and St. Augustine, came upon an amazing sight. A portion of a ship's hull, measuring almost 50 feet or 15 m in length, had unexpectedly washed ashore with the previous night's high tide. Word quickly spread, and within a few hours archaeologists at the Lighthouse Archaeological Maritime Program (LAMP) at the St. Augustine Lighthouse & Maritime Museum were notified about the wreck by a Florida Fish and Wildlife Commission officer. Within 30 minutes, as LAMP prepared for a site inspection, the story broke on the local media. Upon arrival, LAMP archaeologists began a multi-day effort to document the shipwreck remains while also conducting media relations, public archaeology, and organizing an ultimately successful effort to move the beached remains to a safer location for prolonged study and public display (Ropp, this volume).

The wreckage was named the Spring Break Wreck due to the timing of its sudden arrival and its proclivity to attract masses of people to the beach (local law enforcement estimated as many as 1,000 people per day were visiting the wreckage). It consists of a portion of the starboard side of a relatively large, ocean-going sailing vessel, from around 5 ft. above the waterline to around the turn of the bilge. The hull remains were remarkably well-preserved when initially encountered, with deterioration through erosion and marine organisms present only at the uppermost extent of the framing. It was apparent that most or all of this hull segment had been fully submerged and buried in sediment, with just the uppermost ends of its timbers exposed or periodically exposed, from the time of wrecking to its recent and rapid deposition on the beach. Once on the beach, however, the hull remains began to visibly deteriorate, becoming increasingly worse the longer they were exposed to sun and air.

The articulated hull when first observed was comprised of one or more partnered timbers from each of a total of 14 frames (numbered by the original shipwrights 18-31 using Roman numerals) along with the partial remains of seven strakes of ceiling planking and 13 strakes of outer hull planking. Several interesting idiosyncrasies were observed during the recording of the hull, including the aforementioned use of Roman numerals, and also spacer pieces used to separate paired frame members, and square pegs forced through round holes to transversely fasten them. This paper describes the hull remains and provides a preliminary analysis, while serving as an introduction for Burke and Newsom's (this volume) analysis of timber species identification and broader discussion of the geographic, economic, and cultural circumstances from which this vessel originated.

Figure 1 shows a plan view of the hull remains with various members labeled. This is a reconstructed view of the hull as it appeared on the first day of its discovery, based on 3D photogrammetric modeling conducted that day, along with a traditionally recorded hull plan produced on the following day, by which time a number of timbers originally articulated had been torn free and washed away by the rising tide (Ropp, this volume, Figure 2).

Outer Hull Planking

The exterior of a ship's hull was covered with strakes or rows of planking whose purpose was to keep water outside the ship. Thirteen strakes of outer hull planking survived on the wreck when first discovered. Researchers numbered these strakes 1 through 13 from lowest in the hull to highest (Figure 1). It is not clear if some strakes on the hull remnant featured more than one plank, with joins that might have been hidden by frames and planking, because the opportunities to view the hull from below were very limited. The original ends of many of these planks, however, are visible on either side of the wreckage, displaying simple butt joins (Steffy 1994:Figure G11b). Hull planking was fastened to the frames with both wooden treenails and iron planking spikes, described in more detail in a subsequent section below. No caulking or waterproofing agent was observed in the hull planking seams.

As it is believed that the Spring Break Wreck represents a section of hull spanning from above the waterline down to around the turn of the bilge, and the lowermost hull planks were missing, it is probably accurate to refer to the extant outer hull planks as side planking rather than bottom planking (Desmond 1919:57). The outer hull planks below the waterline were southern yellow pine, while those from above the waterline were a hardwood, most likely American beech (Burke and Newsom this volume). Desmond (1919:19) notes that according to Lloyd's insurance standards, beech side planks were rated for only six years, while yellow pine side planks were rated for an even shorter lifetime, five years. This disparity was exacerbated below the waterline, where beech garboard or bottom planks were rated for 12 years while their yellow pine equivalents were considered viable for only half that time (Desmond 1919:19). Saw marks visible on some of the planks were identified as originating from a circular sawmill and a band sawmill, the latter which helps date the site to the 1880s or later (Burke and Newsom, this volume).

Table 1 displays the width and thickness of each hull plank. The average thickness of the hull planks is 2.89 in., and they range in width from 7.09 to 10 in., averaging 8.44 in. Stone (1993:22) relates that large ships used planks more than 11 in. in width, while medium vessels had planks between 8 and 11 in, though he does not define a "large" or "medium" ship by either tonnage or length. Desmond (1919:Table 3B) provides a Lloyd's scantling table, which indicates the average thickness of the outer hull planking on Spring Break Wreck might imply a ship of between 200 and 300 tons, while the dimensions of the thickest plank might indicate a ship of between 300 and 400 tons.

Plank	Width (cm)	Thickness (cm)	Width (in.)	Thickness (in.)
Outer Hull Plank 1	25.4	7.2	10.00	2.83
Outer Hull Plank 2	25.4	7.5	10.00	2.95
Outer Hull Plank 3	25.5	6.6	10.04	2.60
Outer Hull Plank 4	22.4	6.9	8.82	2.72
Outer Hull Plank 5	19.7	6.9	7.76	2.72
Outer Hull Plank 6	20.2	7.5	7.95	2.95
Outer Hull Plank 7	23.1	7.5	9.09	2.95
Outer Hull Plank 8	19.7	6.4	7.76	2.52
Outer Hull Plank 9	20.5	n/a	8.07	n/a
Outer Hull Plank 10	20.1	8.9	7.91	3.50
Outer Hull Plank 11	18.9	n/a	7.44	n/a
Outer Hull Plank 12	18.0	7.9	7.09	3.11
Outer Hull Plank 13	19.8	n/a	7.80	n/a
Ceiling Plank AA	22.5	12.2	8.86	4.80
Ceiling Plank BB	30.5	9.1	12.01	3.58
Ceiling Plank CC	30.7	n/a	12.09	n/a
Ceiling Plank DD	28.8	9.2	11.34	3.62
Ceiling Plank EE	29.5	8.4	11.61	3.31
Ceiling Plank FF	32.3	10.1	12.72	3.98
Ceiling Plank GG	31.2	n/a	12.28	n/a

TABLE 1: Dimensions of planking, Spring Break Wreck.

Ceiling Planking

Ceiling planks are longitudinal interior planks attached to the inboard surfaces of the frames. They make up a floor for the cargo hold, helping to prevent damage to the frames from the moving of heavy cargo, and provide additional longitudinal strength for the hull. Seven strakes of ceiling planking were present on the Spring Break Wreck when first encountered. These were labeled AA through GG, from lowest in the hull to highest (easternmost to westernmost) (Figure 1). Each strake consisted of a single extant or partially extant plank, except for strake FF which featured a long plank terminating in a sizable hook scarf, with the limited remnants of a second plank abaft the scarf join (Figure 2).

The hook scarf appears similar to the standard example illustrated by Steffy (1994:Figure G11b) except that only one end (aft) is indented, while the forward end is simply obliquely cut with no indentation, similar to what Steffy (1994:Figure G11b) calls a diagonal scarf or diagonal butt, or what Desmond (1919:40) terms a "plain" scarf. The scarf is not wedged or keyed at the center, but is indented there. It would be quite secure and resistant to slippage, but not as much as it would be with both ends indented or with a central key (Desmond 1919:40-41). The planks making up this scarfed strake were thicker and wider than their counterparts on adjacent strakes, though the thickest plank was the bottommost, AA, which at 4.8 in. was considerably thicker than all other ceiling, which averaged 3.62 in. (Table 1).

The ceiling planks are quite robust compared to hull planking, which is not uncommon. The averaged ceiling dimensions compared with the Lloyd's scantling table in Desmond (1919:Table 3B) seem to indicate a vessel much larger than would be indicated by the outer hull thickness (900 to 1050 tons compared to 200 to 400 tons). A better comparison seems to be in a second table

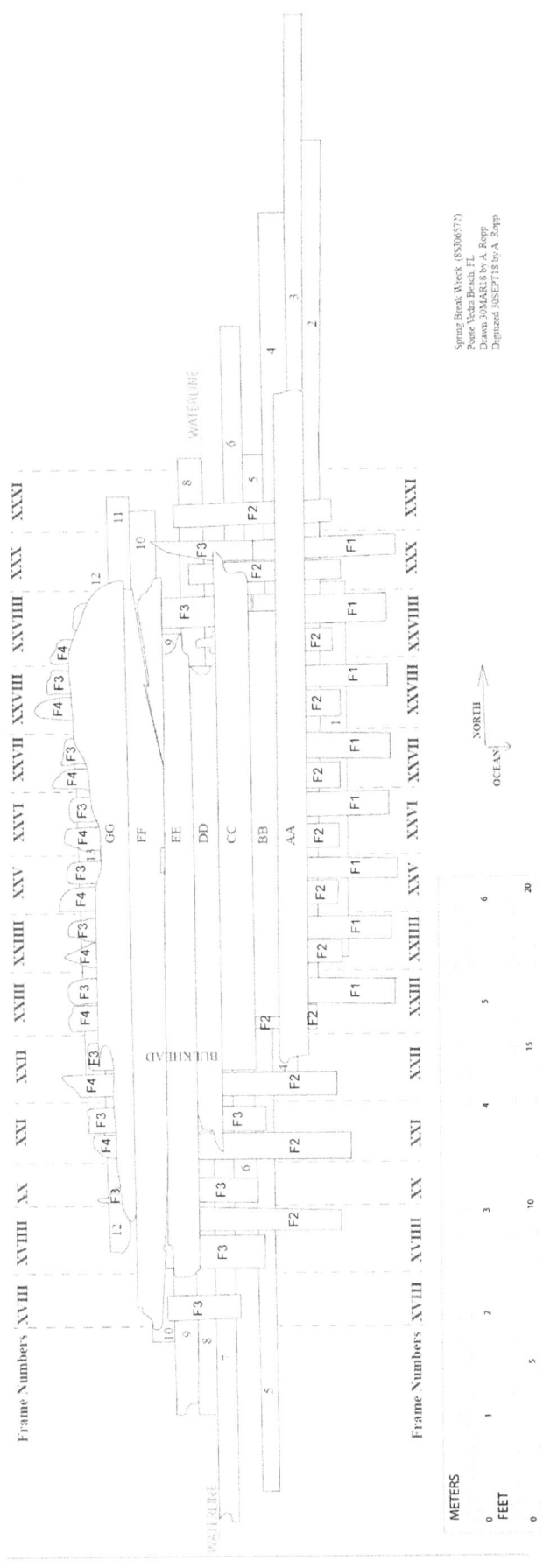

FIGURE 1: Hull plan of the Spring Break Wreck with various hull members labeled. This is a reconstructed view to include timbers observed, but not recorded to scale, on the day of its discovery, since these timbers were disarticulated and lost to tidal action that night, before the remaining hull could be recorded to scale. Illustration by Allyson Ropp and Chuck Meide, courtesy of LAMP.

provided by Desmond (1919:Table 3E), showing "dimensions of parts taken for ships now under construction." The ceiling planks compared to those specified in this table for "above bilge" suggest a ship of between 250 and 350 tons, more consistent with the ship tonnage suggested by the hull planking size.

Various marks were visible on the upper ceiling surfaces. Some were tool marks, from dressing with an adze. Archaeologists surmised that the ship was likely to have sunk while relatively new, before years of cargo loading and offloading had a chance to fully obscure these construction marks. There was also a small, rectangular area on the longer plank in Strake FF which initially appeared to be a repair piece. Closer inspection revealed that this was a small section, around 8 in. by 2 in., where wood

FIGURE 2: Detail of the northwest extent of ceiling planking, showing the scarf in Ceiling Strake FF. Top of the picture is west. Photograph courtesy of LAMP.

had been cut out from the edge of the plank to make it level with the adjacent plank. Some chisel marks were visible from this activity, which was presumably done to seat a beam, knee, or similar feature which straddled the plank seam. A small remnant of this timber survived in the cut area, along with a fastener hole, and a partial impression of where it had been seated was observed on the adjacent plank below, EE. Another feature discernable on the inner surface of the ceiling planking was the impression from what appears to have been a thwartship bulkhead. Its general position is depicted in Figure 1, between Frames 22 and 23. The impression was not clear enough to estimate the dimensions or exact nature of the bulkhead, but it likely was fashioned of wooden planks that ran transversely across the ceiling planking to compartmentalize the cargo hold.

Also visible on the ceiling planking, at the butt end of Ceiling Plank CC, were a series of round impressions made with a large mallet or sledge. These were on the end face of the plank, not the upper surface, and presumably resulted from an attempt to hammer this plank into place from one side. The head of this sledge was around 2 in. in diameter.

The ceiling planks were attached to the frames with both wedged treenails and iron fasteners, discussed in further detail below.

Frames

Frames are the curved timbers which form the skeleton of the ship, defining hull shape and providing the structure to which the outer hull planking is fastened. In traditional Euro-American shipbuilding, each frame is "built-up" or comprised of several individual pieces that are fastened to each other to form a U-shape reflecting the hull cross-section. These built-up frames are then erected on the keel and planked. The bottommost members, which cross the keel, are termed floors, and their outboard ends or wrongheads are connected to a series of overlapping futtocks numbered from lowest to highest (first futtock, second futtock, etc.) and then finally terminating in top timbers. Given the hull remnant's original position within the ship, it is clear that no floors have survived, and it is thus impossible to be able to accurately label the extant futtocks as first, second, etc., since their relationship to the floors is unknown. Likewise it is not certain if the uppermost surviving frame members are top timbers or upper futtocks. For simplicity's sake they will be referred to here as futtocks or frame members.

LAMP researchers have used the same numbering system for the frames that the original shipwrights did, as the frame numbers were inscribed on each timber in the form of Roman numerals. One to four futtocks each from Frames 18 to 31 survived on the hull when initially cast ashore. The individual frame members have been designated Futtock 1, Futtock 2, Futtock 3, and Futtock 4 for each numbered frame (Figure 1). These may not correspond to the original first, second, third, and fourth futtocks, but they allow a system to identify each extant frame member.

As with most large vessels, this ship was double-framed, which means each frame was formed from paired members fastened side by side (Figure 3). While this usually entails bolting the paired members together (Stone 1993:20), on the Spring Break Wreck hull there was a deliberate space or gap between paired frame members. This gap was maintained through the

FIGURE 3: Detail of the lowermost surviving portion of the Spring Break Wreck hull between Frames 28 and 31, facing west or towards the waterline, showing futtocks articulated to hull and ceiling planking, and the gaps and spacer blocks between paired futtocks. Courtesy of LAMP.

repeated use of spacer blocks fashioned from shipyard offcuts, measuring around ¾ in. thick (Figure 3). Paired futtocks were transversely fastened, but instead of using metal bolts, the usual practice, square pegs cut from hardwood were utilized. These were similar in size to the ubiquitous treenails, except that they were squared rather than rounded, and they were cut from beech rather than white oak (Burke and Newsom, this volume). Like the treenails, however, they were driven through pre-augured round holes, which pierced adjacent futtocks and sometimes the spacer blocks between them. This use of squared wooden fasteners driven through round holes has not been observed elsewhere by LAMP archaeologists. While it may seem counterintuitive or even a cliché to force a square peg through a round hole, this arrangement clearly worked to hold paired futtocks together in place until they were more firmly sandwiched between outer hull and inner ceiling. The transverse wooden fasteners, unlike the treenails driven through hull planking, did not need to be watertight, and would have been easier to make than a rounded treenail. What is more, the squared corners of the pegs would also bite or lodge against the augured hole and securely hold the futtocks in position, in what was likely a more effective way of keeping them from twisting out of place during the planking process. Sloane (1965:37) relates that squared wooden fasteners driven into round holes were sometimes used in early colonial house construction when assembling a timber frame, another application where timbers were required to be held together without shifting and where watertight seals were unnecessary.

The use of spaces between paired frame members is relatively rare in shipwreck archaeology literature, and has been observed in several 16th-18th century shipwrecks (Maarleveld 1998a, 1998b; Morris 1996; Steffy 1994: 171; Switzer 1998). The practice seems to be more common in the 19th century, and variations of this arrangement have been seen on both sailing and steam-powered ships from this era (Atkinson and Nash 1987; Gulf Engineers and Tidewater 1992; Meide 2001, 2010; Simmons and Duff 1996: 34-41, 61-63). It appears that the purpose of these spaces was to provide ventilation to promote air flow in the lower hull, and to pack rock salt in the hull, to prevent rot and microbial growth. To resist decay and add years to their working lives, Desmond (1919:103), along with contemporary marine insurance companies, encouraged the salting of wooden vessels.

As has been mentioned previously, the shipwrights had numbered the frames on this vessel, presumably starting at the bow with Frame 1 (Roman numeral "I") towards the stern for some unknown distance beyond Frame 31 (XXXI), the aftermost surviving frame. The Roman numerals were scribed on the inside molded faces of paired frame members, facing each other and thus not easily visible once fastened together as a built-up frame, even before being covered by planking. The sequence of these numbers is the basis for the interpretation of vessel orientation, i.e., that the bow was to the south as the wreckage was first found, and that the wreckage therefore represents the starboard side of the vessel.

There was a deliberate pattern of wood species used for framing. It was observed that futtocks alternated between hardwoods and softwoods. It has since been determined (Burke and Newsom, this volume) that above the waterline, the forward futtocks in paired frames (i.e., Futtock 4 in each frame) were fashioned from beech, while their aft partners (Futtock 3 in each frame) were identified as white pine. There was a transition in this pattern around the waterline, so that both paired futtocks below (i.e., Futtocks 1 and 2 in each frame) were crafted from beech. Burke and Newsom (this volume) also noted that both species appear to have been cut from juvenile trees. Additionally, tool marks from both a hand adze and bandsaw were observed on the futtocks. Burke and Newsom (this volume) have interpreted this as the results of processing tree trunks by hand, and then finalizing the futtocks by bandsaw. They discuss this and other species and processing insights in their paper.

Table 2 shows the scantlings or dimensions of selected individual frame members which could be accurately measured. Their average sided dimension is 9.45 in., and average molded dimension 7.31 in. It is interesting that the molded dimensions of the frame pieces are

Frame Member	Sided (cm)	Molded (cm)	Sided (in.)	Molded (in.)
Frame 18, Futtock 3	24.0	17	9.45	6.69
Frame 19, Futtock 3	27.0	17.5	10.63	6.89
Frame 20, Futtock 3	24.0	18.75	9.45	7.38
Frame 21, Futtock 3	26.0	18.5	10.24	7.28
Frame 22, Futtock 3	26.8	19.5	10.55	7.68
Frame 23, Futtock 1	24.4	18	9.61	7.09
Frame 24, Futtock 1	24.6	18.3	9.69	7.20
Frame 25, Futtock 1	24.3	19.5	9.57	7.68
Frame 26, Futtock 1	22.5	18.3	8.86	7.20
Frame 27, Futtock 1	22.4	18.7	8.82	7.36
Frame 28, Futtock 1	22.9	19.3	9.02	7.60
Frame 29, Futtock 1	22.5	20	8.86	7.87
Frame 30, Futtock 1	22.0	19.8	8.66	7.80
Frame 31, Futtock 2	22.5	16.7	8.86	6.57

TABLE 2: Dimensions of selected frame members, Spring Break Wreck.

smaller than the sided dimensions. This is not usually the case, though it has been observed on other 19th-century shipwrecks (Meide 2001). These dimensions do not readily lend themselves to a comparison with contemporary insurance standard scantlings, as the dimensions listed for example in Desmond (1919:Table 3B and 3E) show sizes for particular hull members such as floors, first futtocks, top timbers, etc., and in some cases call for squared dimensions. Averaging the Spring Break Wreck timbers' sided and molded dimensions and comparing them to a second futtock in Desmond's table of Lloyd's scantlings suggests a ship of around 300 to 400 tons (1919:Table 3B). Likewise, averaging the sided and molded dimensions of a floor and top timber as listed in Desmond (1919:Table 3E) and comparing them to the average of the sided and molded dimensions of the Spring Break Wreck futtocks suggests a ship sized between 250 and 350 tons.

The timber and space (also known as room and space) of the vessel, the distance from the fore side of one frame to the fore side of the following frame (thus including the width or sided dimensions of one frame—both paired futtocks—along with the empty space between it and the next frame), ranged between 23.23 in. and 27.56 in. (59 and 70 cm). This scantling can be compared directly to that mandated in contemporary insurance standards. According to the Lloyd's scantling table included in Desmond (1919:Table 3B) this range indicates a ship of more than 200 and less than 500 tons. A second table provided by Desmond (1919:Table 3E), which relates scantlings "for ships now under construction" provides similar results, suggesting a size between 250 and 450 tons.

Fasteners and Fastening Patterns

The outer hull planks were fastened to the frames with wooden treenails and also with ½ in. square-shanked iron spikes. Many treenails were driven through both ceiling and hull planks and the frames in between, and then wedged at each end. Others were blind treenails, driven through the ceiling into the inboard surface of the frame, or from hull planking into the outboard surface of the frame, in neither case protruding at the far end. This situation is typical, according to Desmond (1919:58-59), who wrote that "many of the fastenings go through outer plank, frame, and inner plank. . . . [however, a]s the inside planking (ceiling) is not laid at the same time that outside planking is a certain proportion of both outer and inner planking fastenings must be driven into frames only." All originally exposed treenail ends were wedged. The typical diameter of the Spring Break Wreck treenails is around 1.18 in. (roughly the equivalent of 1 11/64 in.). This is close to the size of treenails that Desmond (1919:3F) lists as being used for ships between 150 and 900 tons, which is 1 1/8 in.

There were also iron bolts driven through the ceiling planking, which did not appear to protrude beyond the frames. The impressions of at least one clench ring associated with these iron fasteners were visible on the upper surface of ceiling planking, though for the most part the form and size of these fasteners are obscured by concretion.

At either end of the hull remains, there were lengths of exposed hull planking unobscured by frame members, where a fastener pattern could be discerned. The hull appears to be double fastened, featuring two fasteners through each hull plank at each frame. An alternating pattern was observed, at least on several of the exposed hull planks at the northern (aftermost) end of the wreckage, whereby the forward paired frame member featured two treenails, and its aft partner had one treenail and one iron fastener. This arrangement does not conform exactly to Desmond's (1919:59-60) definitions of single fastening, double fastening, or alternative fastening. He relates that "larger wooden vessels were nearly always double fastened, medium ones were double fastened above the water and alternate fastened below, and the smaller ones were alternate fastened above and single fastened below" (1919:59). At the butt joins, each plank end featured one treenail, usually roughly centered but sometimes offset, with two iron planking spikes closer to the join.

Copper Alloy Sheathing

While opportunities to inspect the lower surface of the hull remains were limited, it became readily apparent that the bottom of the hull had been coppered. Applying overlapping sheets of copper or a specific copper alloy to the outer hull below the waterline was a standard practice in the 19th century, to protect wooden ships from the detrimental effects of shipworms (Staniforth 1984). Most of the sheeting and tacks are gone, though in various places tiny scraps of sheathing can be observed clinging to the occasional remaining tack. Where they could be observed, the sheathing tack holes showed no evidence of added repair pieces or of re-coppering. This is another indicator that the ship wrecked as a relatively young vessel.

Another important piece of evidence revealed by inspection of sheathing tack holes was the position of the waterline on the hull. The upper edge of the copper or copper alloy sheathing was identified as running approximately in line with the seam between Outer Hull Planks 7 and 8, and is indicated in Figure 1.

It was also noted that, despite the copper alloy sheathing, the hull planks were fastened with iron spikes. It was well known by the 19th century that iron fasteners under copper sheathing suffered catastrophic deterioration from the galvanic action of two dissimilar metals in contact in seawater, so this is somewhat surprising. The normal and more expensive practice was to use copper alloy plank fastenings, but at the very least American Lloyd's mandated that, if iron spikes had to be used, they should be countersunk one inch and plugged with pine (Meyer and Salter 1883:xvii), a practice that was not followed here.

Shipwright's Marks

The Roman numeral frame numbering system used by the shipwrights to identify individual frame members and associate them with particular frames has already been described above. It is somewhat reminiscent to the numbering system that was used on the 17th-century ship *la Belle,* which originally had been meant to be shipped to the New World disarticulated for assembly upon its destination (Bruseth et al. 2017). The use of a similar system here implies timbers were cut to a predetermined form and labeled for later assembly.

These were not the only scribed markings left by the shipbuilders. Another one, whose function remains unknown, appears as a series of diagonal lines somewhat like a modern hashtag symbol. At least three diagonal lines are crossed by another set of opposing 5 diagonal lines. These are scribed into the inner surface of a hull plank underneath Frame 29, where a missing futtock or possibly floor would have been (Figure 3). It is not known if this had a construction-related function or if it might have been graffiti.

An additional symbol was scratched into the forward surface of Frame 30, Futtock 1. It appears to be an arrow pointing downwards at the lower edge of Hull Plank 2. It is not known if this was meant to help position the frame member over a particular planking seam, or if it served some other purpose.

Discussion

The Spring Break Wreck represents a significant portion of the starboard side of an ocean-going, wooden sailing vessel, spanning from around 5 ft. above the waterline to about 6 ft. below the waterline and around the turn of the bilge. It was likely a bulk cargo carrying vessel, perhaps a schooner, built in the 1880s-1890s. Figure 4 shows the midship section of such a schooner with the cross-section of the hull remains superimposed to scale in their approximate position. While this is not a perfect method for use in reconstructing the size and shape of the original vessel, the curvature and waterline of the hull remnant line up rather well with those on the drawn section. With the midship section scaled to fit the hull remains, the breadth of this hypothetical reconstruction measures around 32 ft. Given most ships' length to beam ratio is between 1:3 and 1:5, this breadth would suggest a vessel length of between 96 and 160 ft. The schooner depicted in Figure 4, built in East Boothbay, Maine, in the early 20th century, is of comparable size, measuring 152 ft. on deck with a breadth of 33 ft. and depth of hold of 12 ½ ft (Desmond 1919:197).

In preceding sections of this paper, period scantlings tables were used to generate tonnage estimates for the Spring Break ship, based on planking thickness, treenail diameter, and frame dimensions and spacing. There was some variety in these estimates, between 200 and 500 tons. Averaging these various tonnage ranges results in an estimate of between 240 and 408 tons. According to Desmond (1919:Table 3E), a generic 350-ton vessel has a length between perpendiculars of 145 ft., extreme breadth of 25 ft., and a hold depth of 13 ft., while a 450-ton vessel has a length of 145 ft., breadth of 33 ft., and hold depth of 13 ft. It seems likely that the Spring Break ship, judging from the superimposition in Figure 4 and the averaged scantlings estimates, would have been comparable in size with these estimates.

Following Ropp's (this volume) overview of the discovery and recovery of this shipwreck, this paper serves as an introduction to understanding the basic construction of the Spring Break Wreck hull, and offers a simple model of reconstruction to estimate its original size. The work of Burke and Newsom, in this volume, continues this analysis with a broader discussion of the sociocultural and economic context behind the construction of this ship, and its possible geographic origins, and a more in depth scrutiny of the species and characteristics of the woods and tools used in its construction. The Spring Break Wreck, with its sometimes peculiar and idiosyncratic hull features, some of which may indicate vernacular origins, has proven to be an interesting example among the multitude of 19th-century shipwrecks that have been examined by archaeologists, and continued research promises to reveal even more about this unique vessel built between the twilight of wooden sail and the dawn of modernity.

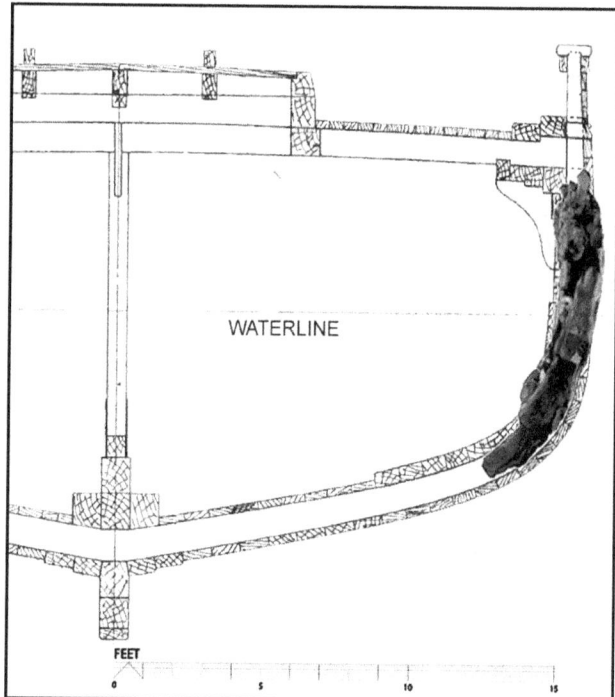

FIGURE 4: The midship section of a 152-ft. auxiliary schooner, designed by John G. Alden and built in East Boothbay, Maine ca. 1919, with a photomodel of the Spring Break Wreck hull remains superimposed in what would be their approximate position in a hull of this type. The midship section has been scaled to match the size of the hull remains, and thus shows the hypothetical dimension and shape of the original Spring Break vessel. Illustration by Chuck Meide, midship section from Desmond 1919:197, photomodel courtesy of LAMP.

Acknowledgments

The investigation of the Spring Break Wreck was funded by the St. Augustine Lighthouse & Maritime Museum, local donations, and a grant from the Division of Historical Resources, Florida Department of State through the Florida Historical Commission. The timbers were recorded with the help of FPAN, SEARCH, USF, and LAMP volunteers, and moved from the beach with donated equipment and expertise from Construction Debris Removal, Inc. and St. Augustine City Commissioner John Valdes, along with GTM Research Reserve and Florida Bureau of Archaeological Research staff.

References

ATKINSON, KAREN AND MICHAEL NASH
1987 Report on the excavation of the *Hadda*. *Bulletin of the Australian Institute for Maritime Archaeology* 11(2):17-24.

BRUSETH, JAMES E., AMY A. BORGENS, BRADFORD M. JONES AND ERIC D. RAY (EDITORS)
2017 *La Belle: The Archaeology of a Seventeenth-Century Ship of New World Colonization*. Texas A&M University Press, College Station.

DESMOND, CHARLES
1919 *Wooden Ship-Building*. The Rudder Publishing Company, New York.

GULF ENGINEERS & CONSULTANTS, INC. AND TIDEWATER ATLANTIC RESEARCH
1992 *Archeological Documentation and Testing of a Mid-Nineteenth Century Tugboat at Hutchinson Island, Savannah, Chatham County, Georgia*. Report prepared by Gulf Engineers & Consultants, Inc. and Tidewater Atlantic Research, and submitted to the U.S. Army Corps of Engineers, Savannah District.

MAARLEVELD, THIJS
1998a *Archaeology and Early Modern Merchant Ships: Building Sequence and Consequences, an Introductory Review*. In *Archaeological Heritage Management in Dutch Waters: Exploratory Studies*, edited by T. Maarleveld, pp. 81-103. Scheepsarcheologie V. Nederlands Institut voor Scheeps- en onderwwaterArcheologie/ROB(NISA), Lelystad.

1998b Double-Dutch Solutions in Flush-Planked Shipbuilding: Continuity and Adaptations at the Start of Modern History. In *Archaeological Heritage Management in Dutch Waters: Exploratory Studies*, edited by T. Maarleveld, pp. 121-133. Scheepsarcheologie V. Nederlands Institut voor Scheeps- en onderwwaterArcheologie/ROB(NISA), Lelystad.

MEIDE, CHUCK
2001 The Archaeology of Economic Transition: the Excavation of the San Marcos Shipwreck, a Mid-Nineteenth Century Merchant Sailing Ship Lost at St. Marks, Florida. Unpublished Master's thesis, Department of Anthropology, Florida State University, Tallahassee.

2010 The Excavation of an Unidentified Sailing Vessel Lost on the Nineteenth Century North Breakers off St. Augustine, Florida: Results of the 2009 Field Season. In *ACUA Underwater Archaeology Proceedings 2010*, edited by C. Horrell and M. Damour, pp. 17-29. Advisory Council on Underwater Archaeology, Amelia Island, Florida.

MEYER, H. F. A. AND C. FREDERICK SALTER
1883 *American Lloyd's Register of American and Foreign Shipping*. Charles Vogt, New York, New York. <https://research.mysticseaport.org/item/l0237571883/9/>. Accessed 5 March 2019.

MORRIS, JOHN WILLIAM III
1996 Shipwreck 44YO88: the Hull. In *Final Report on the Yorktown Shipwreck Archaeological Project*, edited by J. Broadwater, pp. 61-105. National Endowment for the Humanities, Williamsburg, Virginia.

SIMMONS, JOE J. III AND JAMES A. DUFF
1996 *Phase II Archaeological Data Recovery, Area 4, Fig Island Channel Site, Savannah Harbor, Savannah, Georgia*. Report prepared by Panamerican Consultants, Inc., and submitted to the U.S. Army Corps of Engineers, Savannah District, and Gulf Engineers & Consultants, Inc.

SLOANE, ERIC
1965 *A Reverence for Wood*. Funk and Wagnalls, New York.

STANIFORTH, MARK
1984 The Introduction and Use of Copper Sheathing -- A History. *Bulletin of the Australian Insitute for Maritime Archaeology* 9(1 & 2):21-48.

STEFFY, J. RICHARD
1994 *Wooden Ship Building and the Interpretation of Shipwrecks*. Texas A&M University Press, College Station.

STONE, DAVID LEIGH
1993 *The Wreck Diver's Guide to Sailing Ship Artifacts of the 19th Century*. Underwater Archaeological Society of British Columbia, Vancouver, British Columbia.

SWITZER, DAVID C.
1998 The Defence, 1779. In *Excavating Ships of War*, edited by M. Bound, pp. 182-193. Anthony Nelson, Oswestry, Shropshire.

• • • • • • • • • • • • • • • •

Chuck Meide
Lighthouse Archaeological Maritime Program (LAMP)
St. Augustine Lighthouse & Maritime Museum
81 Lighthouse Avenue
St Augustine, FL 32080
cmeide@staugustinelighthouse.org

A Square Peg in a Round Hole: Wood Analysis from the Spring Break Wreck

Brendan Burke & Lee Newsom

This paper discusses results of wood analysis performed on samples taken from the Spring Break Wreck (8SJ6572), articulated late-19th century vessel remains that washed up on Ponte Vedra Beach, Florida. Analysis included taxonomic assignments of individual hull components, along with observations on tree age, growth form, and growth-ring characteristics as they relate to timber/lumber production. We consider species selection, economy of wood use, and possible location of ship construction based on materials sourcing. An attempt is made to identify landscape changes that may have affected the cultural milieu of the shipwright, influencing building methods and changing longstanding maritime traditions.

Introduction

Examination of historic shipwreck timbers can provide unique glimpses into human interaction with past environments. Close inspection offers clues about wood sourcing, selection, and processing. Taxonomic assignment, growth form, processing, and placement are each indicative of a shipbuilder's knowledge, skill, association with technology, and accessibility to raw materials. Synthetic analysis of these factors, when available, can be helpful to assign cultural affiliation, use, and temporality of an historic vessel. In this paper, tentative conclusions are presented from analysis of wood components of the Spring Break Wreck (8SJ6572).

Residents of South Ponte Vedra Beach encountered historic shipwreck debris during a morning beach walk on 28 March, 2018. A segment of wooden hull had washed ashore during the previous night's high tide and was stranded in the upper tidal zone. The wreckage was reported to local law enforcement. Officers from the St. Johns County Sheriff's Office responded to the scene and alerted archaeologists with the St. Augustine Lighthouse Archaeological Maritime Program (LAMP). A LAMP recording team dispatched to the site and began assessment, recordation, and ultimately relocation of the large fragment of historic shipwreck debris. Measuring nearly fifty feet in length, wreckage attracted attention from beachgoers, whose numbers were increased by tourists visiting the area during spring break. Media attention drove additional site visitation and by 30 March, local law enforcement reported over one thousand vehicles per day visiting the site.

Due to increased pressure from site visitation, unique issues were presented to resource managers and recording archaeologists such as visitation access, site interpretation, and whether or not to relocate the wreckage. While these matters were being settled, LAMP archaeologists began recordation to triage the site in preparation for washing back out to sea, damage from wave action, or purposed relocation. Recordation began by photographing the site for 3D rendering, gathering basic measurements of hull components, and taking wood samples from representative timbers. During the first night, wreckage was moved by the tide and badly damaged; an entire row of futtocks, planking, and ceiling timbers was torn away. During the second day of recordation, the site was strapped to screw anchors placed around the timbers to prevent further movement. The third and fourth days on site included additional wood sampling, completion of a site plan, measurement of scantlings, and additional public archaeology to provide site interpretation for visitors.

Sampling Strategy and Identification

Recovering wood samples from shipwrecked timbers is a process requiring careful consideration of environmental factors affecting wood up to, and during time of sampling. Once taken, curation of wood samples is critical to retain integrity for laboratory analysis. Wood from shipwrecks passes through a number of phases prior to sampling, including growth, harvesting, processing, possible curing, damage from use while part of the vessel (fire, abrasion, tearing, splitting), damage from the wrecking process, environmental degradation while submerged (mineral staining, long-period immersion, mechanical abrasion from unsettled sediments, shipworm damage, damage from looters), and deterioration from drying out. Any of these factors may render macro examination of wood for purposes of taxonomic classification tenuous at best and can misidentify species similar in appearance (e.g., beech and oak, the confamilial genera *Fagus* and *Quercus*, respectively).

Wood samples were collected from each type of hull component at the Spring Break Wreck. Samples were extracted using a hand-powered metal pull-saw and sample location was photographically recorded. Hull components such as futtocks and ceiling timbers were individually identified in case of species mixing within a type of hull component such as a scarphed timber. Where possible, samples attempted to capture several cubic centimeters of wood to allow for examination of transverse, tangential, and radial surfaces.

Each sample was initially examined, including those with multiple specimens, to inspect for the general condition and preservation state of the wood, upon which specific locations across the exposed surfaces were selected for thin section removal and analysis. Translucent thin sections were taken using a stainless-steel microtome blade, drawing from each of the three diagnostic planes of reference (cross or transverse [xs], radial longitudinal [rls]). The sections were wet-mounted on glass microscope slides under glass cover slips in a 50% glycerin solution, then examined under magnifications ranging from 40 to 600x using an Olympus BX51 compound microscope.

Anatomical observations were recorded according to International Association of Wood Anatomists (IAWA) standards (IAWA Committee 1989, 2004). The individual wood taxonomic assignments were made using published keys, with emphasis on North American commercial woods (Panshin and de Zeeuw 1980), and by means of the online resource (*InsideWood* 2004-onwards; Wheeler 2011). A comparative slide collection was used to verify taxonomic assignments. All samples were assigned to the lowest possible taxonomic rank. A total of twenty-three field samples were collected from the Spring Break Wreck.

Analysis of ecological and functional anatomical variation may indicate the origin of wood within a tree, such as trunk versus branch, and tree response to environmental factors such as droughts or hurricanes. For example, conifers develop "compression wood," a form of "reaction wood," on the underside of branches and leaning stems. Likewise, hardwoods (Angiosperms) may develop another form of reaction wood known as "tension wood" specifically on the upper surfaces of branches and leaning stems. Western shipbuilding traditions during the modern age (1500-present) frequently sourced curved timbers, when available, to take advantage of the associated differences in mechanical properties, including relative strength and flexibility. Such 'compass' timbers include knees, breasthooks, stems, and futtocks. Where macro analysis may easily identify compass timbers by shape and grain orientation, degradation of shipwreck components may periodically preclude identification. In other words, sample size may be too small to verify original shape. Thus, microanalysis can utilize small sample sizes to possibly indicate timber placement within a tree. Additional indicators, such as juvenile versus mature wood, can indicate utilization of various types of tree (sapling versus mature bole) within specific taxa.

Hull components of the Spring Break wreck were analyzed for processing marks. Similar to taxonomic classification, processing marks are distinguishing marks on wood left by sawmills used to process trees into timbers and boards, or by hand tools used to form and dress lumber. Examples of such are the overlapping, arcing striations left by a circular saw. Alternately, processing timber by hand leaves an irregular, scalloped surface on hewn timbers. In each case, known temporal sequences allow researchers to date a period during which a ship component may have been manufactured. Where observed, these marks were recorded on the Spring Break Wreck and help tell the story of the vessel's history.

Sample Results

Wood samples were taken from outer hull planking, futtocks, ceiling planking, and treenails. Results are categorized by ship component. Three softwoods and two hardwoods were identified (see Table 1). Vernacular names for taxa are used here with scientific nomenclature in parenthesis.

Futtocks

Frames rise from the outward and upward from the keel to give shape and strength to a vessel. Outer hull planking is fastened to the outside of frames to create a watertight layer. On the inside, frames are frequently lined with inner planking called a 'ceiling' to add strength and protect the ship's framework from cargo damage. In constructing vessels of size, where a single, curved wooden frame is impractical or impossible, frames were made as composite units pieced together from individual timbers called futtocks. Futtocks were fastened together and paired with staggered butt joints for strength. Frames in the Spring Break Wreck were comprised of paired, alternating rows of futtocks. Wooden spacer blocks, made from offcuts, were placed between rows of futtocks to create a gap between the

Sample #	Component	Taxonomic Assignment	Specimen Observations/comments
1.1	treenail	*Quercus* sp., white anatomical group	end is split as for placement of a wedge
2.1	frame J (#11 ?), east end	*Fagus* sp.	
3.1	outer hull plank 5	*Pinus* sp., *Taeda* anatomical group	
4.1	ceiling plank 2	*Picea* sp.	
5.1	frame	*Fagus* sp.	quarter sawn timber with holes drilled for five treenails
6.1	treenail	*Fagus* sp.	
7.1	hull plank	*Pinus* sp., *Taeda* anatomical group	
8.1	treenail	*Quercus* sp., white anatomical group	anatomy suggests *Q. alba*, white oak (classic form); fully cut form from mature timber
9.1	frame	*Fagus* sp.	
10.1	ceiling plank	*Pinus* sp., *Strobus* anatomical group	
11.1	ceiling plank	*Pinus* sp., *Strobus* anatomical group	anatomy suggests *P. strobus*, white pine
12.1	frame	*Pinus* sp., *Strobus* anatomical group	rapid growth (juvenile wood), wide rings, few per inch
13.1	frame	*Pinus* sp., *Strobus* anatomical group	timber from relatively young tree, includes pith
14.4	treenail	*Quercus* sp., white anatomical group	cut to form from young growth, i.e., a sapling, based on ring width, curvature & presence of knots
15.1	treenail	*Quercus* sp., white anatomical group	anatomy suggests *Q. alba*, white oak (classic form); cut form, mature wood
16.1	"copper tack"	*Pinus* sp., *Taeda* anatomical group	
17.1	treenail	*Fagus* sp.	cut form with a knot (but appears mature)
18.1	square peg	*Fagus* sp.	cut to form from mature growth with minimal curvature of growth rings; the wide flat edges are tangent to both the rays and the growth rings
19.1	hull plank	*Pinus* sp., *Taeda* anatomical group	plain sawn timber (tangential plank), slow growth (multiple rings per inch)
20.1	frame	*Fagus* sp.	timber from relatively young tree; nearly complete bole segment, including pith, 1/2 bole (trunk split down midline); two lateral surfaces were trimmed/planed flat, truncating a portion of the growth increments [sample is 'D shaped' in xs]
21.1	treenail	*Fagus* sp.	
22.1	concretion	Fagaceae	thin layer of wood in cylindrical form, possible treenail remnant
23.1	concretion	*Fagus* sp.	

TABLE 1: Wood samples from the Spring Break Wreck by vessel component and species.

forward set of futtocks and the after set of futtocks (for further discussion of construction methods, see Meide this volume). Spacing rows of futtocks longitudinally within a single composite frame provides airflow and allows for the addition of salt to prevent the formation of wood-eating microbes. Consideration of airflow in a vessel's lower structure was of increasing concern by shipbuilders and insurers during the nineteenth century (BuShips 1983; Curtis 2009; Desmond 1919). The ventilation space between rows of futtocks in the Spring Break Wreck was approximately 1.90 cm (.75 in.). Frame numbers, as interpreted, were found carved into moulded faces of futtocks. Fourteen paired frames were identified.

Forward futtocks in paired frames were identified as American beech (*Fagus grandiflora*), indicated by samples 2.1, 5.1, 9.1, and 20.1. After-futtocks were identified as white pine (*Pinus strobus*; i.e., the section *Strobus* or white pine wood anatomical group) and indicated by samples 12.1 and 13.1. At a point just below the waterline, both courses of futtocks were cut from beech. Beech futtocks appear to have been cut from juvenile trees as half splits were common among futtocks along with the presence of pith, sometimes including the outer surface of the log (Figure 1). White pine futtocks appear to have been similarly cut from smaller diameter trees with pervasive knots (Figure 2).

Both white pine and beech futtocks exhibited processing marks. Beech, the harder of the two woods retained more pronounced marks including bandsaw marks on upper sided surfaces and adze marks on moulded faces.

Outer Hull Planking

Outer hull planking included the southern yellow pine anatomical group and the beech anatomical group. Three samples, 3.1, 7.1 and 19.1 contained characteristics on the micro and macro level consistent

FIGURE 1: The proximal face of a beech (*Fagus grandiflora*) futtock is shown here. Note the presence of outer tree surface and proximity to pith. (Photo by Brendan Burke 2018.)

FIGURE 2: A treenail projects from the surface of this white pine (*Pinus strobus*) futtock. This course of white pine futtocks was found to begin just below the waterline and extend upwards in the hull. Note the presence of a knot and a pitch pocket, characteristic of the quality of white pine used in Spring Break Wreck framing. (Photo by Brendan Burke, 2018.)

with loblolly pine (*P. taeda*), longleaf pine (*P. palustris*), or slash pine (*P. elliottii*). Pine planking was cut from trees with annular ring density averaging 8-14 rings per inch (Figure 3). Planking below the waterline on this vessel appears to have been from pine, planking above the waterline appears to have been from beech. Processing marks on below-water outer hull planks included two types of cutting, band sawmill and circular sawmill. No processing marks were extant on hardwood planking.

FIGURE 3: A thin section of southern yellow pine (*Pinus sp.*) outer hull planking. The section has been backlit to highlight annular rings. Note the two areas of dark staining caused by nearby iron spikes. (Photo by Brendan Burke, 2019.)

Ceiling Planking

On 28 March seven ceiling planks were intact (see Figure 1 in Meide, this volume). By 29 March two ceiling planks were found detached from the wreck along with a number of futtocks. Of the remaining ceiling, one plank was built with a hook scarph and is thicker and wider than its adjacent ceiling planks. Both sections of the scarph were sampled and were identified as representatives of the spruce (*Picea* sp.) genus. The other ceiling plank (BB) sampled was identified as white pine (*Pinus strobus*), i.e., assigned to the white pine anatomical group (section *Strobus*).

Processing marks visible on ceiling planking were limited to tool marks on the upper surfaces. Although weathered and worn by cargo, the marks appeared to be dressing marks from an adze. No saw marks were visible on plank edges although sledging marks were recorded on the end of one ceiling plank (CC), perhaps evidence of being driven into place during construction.

Treenails

Six samples (1.1, 6.1, 8.1, 14.4, 15.1 and 17.1) of treenails were removed for identification. Four treenails were identified with the white oak anatomical group (*Quercus sp.*). White oak has also been historically considered a first-rate shipbuilding material for keels, planking, and frames (BuShips 1983; Curtis 2009; Desmond 1919) and often used in treenails. However, the Spring Break Wreck did not exhibit any oaken structural components except treenails. Of note, one sample (15.1) indicates utilization of a young tree or oak branch as treenail material. Two treenails (6.1 and 17.1) were identified as American beech (*Fagus grandiflora*) which may indicate repurposing waste material from cutting beech futtocks.

Assembly Fasteners

During original assembly of frame members, floors and futtocks were fastened to each other to create a rigid unit. Typical historic shipbuilding methods call for assembly of a frame member on a framing stage prior to being raised and stepped on the keel (Curtis 2009:49). Since frames were designed with an airway between alternating rows of futtocks, spacer blocks were used to maintain the gap. Through both courses of futtocks, and through the spacer block, holes were bored longitudinally to accept a rectangular beech peg. Sloane (1965) indicates this type of fastener was used traditionally in early colonial house construction when assembling a timber frame. Biting action of square edges in a round hole also provided a sort of keyway to prevent the joined pieces from twisting out of place. This type of fastener would have served a purpose only during vessel construction and was not required to be watertight.

Wood Processing

Saw marks on wood can be critical in assigning processing dates and establishing a life-sequence for a vessel, including the nature of build and subsequent repairs. In the case of the Spring Break Wreck, four distinct types of processing marks were recorded: band sawmill, circular sawmill, bandsaw and adze. The three types of saw marks indicate a high degree of communication with technology yet reveal some limitations of the builder. Understanding lumber markets and wood-processing technology during the nineteenth century is important to place this wreck into context.

Balloon framing house construction, railroad expansion, and factory-made wooden furniture were some of the driving factors for increased lumber demand during the mid-nineteenth century (Clement 2014:34). Enterprising individuals, such as Henry Buck, of Bucksport, Maine, ventured south to wring timber riches out of southeastern forests (McAlister 2013) and southern lumber production began to increase rapidly in 1870 while northeastern lumber output remained relatively flat. During the late 1880s, southern production equaled northeastern output and by 1896 skyrocketed past the nation's most prolific region, the Great Lakes states. Southern lumber production peaked in 1910, when almost eighteen billion board feet of pine and cypress were consigned for shipment. Southern output more than equaled the combined production of the Great Lakes states, the Pacific Coast, and the U.S. northeast (Hoyt 1919:14). Shipbuilders quickly took advantage of the lumber supply and by the end of the nineteenth century Yankee-built ships often included as much southern pine as any other species. The durable, rosin-soaked southern pine found its way into decks, planking, spars, keels, keelsons, and longitudinal architecture (Desmond 1919:16). Shipbuilding in the United States clung to traditional wooden construction while British yards, major competitors in shipping tonnage, switched to iron and steel (Harley 1973). Harley (1973:381) continues, providing the index for wholesale American lumber prices from 1856 to 1886, which increased 0.3 percent per year while the cost of British iron fell during the same period by 3.7 percent per year. The differential left American shipbuilders, excepting a few of the largest builders, building 'practical' vessels throughout the century, as British shipbuilders switched to modern iron hulls (Thiesen 2006:45). Simply, American builders were encouraged to continue to build traditional vessels with cheap materials (Figure 4).

Increased demand of wood products in the United States created a proliferation of sawmills wherever forests stood. Existing water or wind-powered sash sawmills could not keep pace, nor was there ample water or wind

FIGURE 4: This four-masted lumber schooner, *Henry J. Smith*, was photographed in Savannah in 1907 loading lumber. The schooner was built in 1890 by Washburn Brothers Shipyard in Thomaston, Maine. While *Henry J. Smith* was 1108 tons, and likely much larger than the Spring Break Wreck vessel, it would have been constructed similarly. Note the open loading ports on either side of the stem. This type of vessel, built in various sizes, was the workhorse of American coastwise and international shipping during the late nineteenth and early twentieth centuries. (Photo by Detroit Publishing Company; courtesy of the Library of Congress, Washington, D.C.)

power in the southeastern forests. With the advent of portable boilers during the early nineteenth century, steam engines chuffed and circular sawmills snarled throughout the piney woods of the Low Country and Gulf Coast. Circular sawmills, iconic for their large, round blades, cut quickly and offered flexibility in processing logs. A carriage swiftly turned, clamped, and carried a log through the blade. The miller could turn the log between cuts to maximize lumber output and select the type of lumber being cut (eg. flat, rift, or quarter-sawn). Flexibility of cut with a circular mill provided an advantage over the gang or sash sawmills already in use. Those mills, while having clear advantages in labor over the antique human-powered saw pit, simply sliced a log into boards without taking into account orientation of grain. Additionally, sash mills were slow, sometimes producing only a few boards per day. Circular sawmills revolutionized lumber production during the mid-nineteenth century as millions of board feet of lumber could be produced by a single circular mill in a year. However, the big-whirring saws had two distinct disadvantages. First, thick blades used in a circular mill left a wide kerf, the area of wood wasted by the sawblade; good wood ended up as a pile of sawdust. Second, as virgin timber resources of the cypress swamps of Louisiana and softwood forests of the coastal Pacific were cut, huge cypress, redwood, sequoia, spruce, and Douglas fir required larger blades to cut the massive trunks. Inventors throughout the nineteenth century struggled with the concept of an endless steel blade to cut large logs. Running over two wheels, one powered and one an idler, entrepreneurs realized the secret to modern sawmills lay in the band sawmill.

During the 1880s a number of band sawmills became available to lumber producers. A fit of innovation, driven by near-frenetic industry needs and better metallurgy, emboldened manufacturers. The concept of a band sawmill was not new, but heretofore impracticable due to the inability to make band blades that were flexible yet tempered to hold an edge. According to Prescott (1910) early band sawmills were plagued with breakdown, inefficiency, and required hiring additional labor for servicing. Moreover, attempts at developing a successful band sawmill were foiled by the inability to cut straight lumber; improperly tensioned blades followed wood grain and not the desires of millers. The result was 'snaky' lumber unfit for sale and a general distrust of the technology. In 1889, D. Clinton Prescott patented a band sawmill that automatically tensioned the blade according to load and solved the straight cutting problem (Prescott 1910:25). Prescott's mills required less upkeep and could be maintained by mill workers; the band mill problem was solved and just in time.

Outer hull planking in the Spring Break Wreck, cut from southern yellow pine, displays both circular and band sawmill marks. Perhaps the shipyard was in proximity to both types of sawmill and sourced planking opportunistically. It might be expected that a northern yard would have shipped in sufficient planking from a single source to build a vessel. If so, only one type of mill might be represented.

To create futtocks, tree trunks must be processed into blank slabs, or flitches. In the case of the Spring Break Wreck, these flitches appear to have been hand hewn and dressed. Scalloped adze marks were briefly evident on the moulded faces of futtocks, before drying began to alter wood appearance. Cutting futtocks from the flitches utilized a bandsaw, as indicated by saw marks on the sided face of several frames. Similar to a band sawmill, a bandsaw relies upon a continuously moving toothed metal blade and was available to American craftsmen during the late nineteenth century. To handle large flitches a sizeable bandsaw is required. In large shipyards, a ship saw would have served to cut futtocks. A special type of bandsaw, the ship saw can change cutting angle during a cut by rotating the entire cutting mechanism. The angle can be changed during a cut to create a transitional bevel that matches not only the curvature of a hull but taper. Futtock measurements and appearance did not indicate that a ship saw was employed in the preparation of frames. If a standard bandsaw was used, the exterior faces of frames would need to be hand dressed to mate with outer hull planking. Nonetheless, the presence of a bandsaw of sufficient size to mill thick flitches indicates a technical ability of this builder beyond simple hand tools and a possession of a power source for such a machine, either a powered line-shaft or electricity.

Discussion

The Spring Break Wreck vessel was relatively new when lost. Frames and ceiling are devoid of old fastener holes, indicative of repair or replaced hull components. Outer hull planking exhibits only one sequence of coppering, indicating a lack of re-coppering or extensive repair to copper sheathing. With this in mind, a tentative composite view of the vessel and its origins may be formed.

Beech, while suited for furniture, flooring, and tool handles, has been traditionally considered a second class shipbuilding wood, sometimes avoided altogether (BuShips 1983: 20; Desmond 1919; Goodwin 1997). In England, beech was only allowed in shipbuilding for the Royal Navy when oak was not available (Holland 1985). The American Forest Products Laboratory (AFPL 2010:2-4) rates beech with low resistance to wet rot, a reason it was traditionally avoided for use in lower architecture. Desmond (1919:49) rates beech as a substandard replacement in shipbuilding and only recommends its use as a last-resort in false keels, behind oak and hard maple.

Desmond (1919: 9) bemoans the lack of using seasoned wood for shipbuilding by the early twentieth century. If green beech was used in the framing of this ship and paired with white pine, a differential in volumetric shrinkage may have been the beginning of the end for this vessel. According to the USDA Forest Products Laboratory (AFPL 2010:4.2) beech has an average volumetric shrinkage rate of 17.2%. White pine has an average shrinkage rate of approximately 8.2%, a disproportionate shrinkage rate of 2:1. Since paired frames are fastened to the same planks unequal movement of frames during the curing process may have caused premature fastener failure and plank loosening. Beech was used for the two lower courses of framing below the waterline; however the lowest course of white pine overlaps below the waterline and exposes the two dissimilar woods to additional shrinkage/expansion shock.

Many futtocks used for the vessel include knots, often multiple knots per futtock. This attribute weakens timbers and denotes a lesser-grade of wood. Many of the knots in Spring Break Wreck wood were not closed by tree maturation, a weak type of knot to incorporate into a timber and may indicate selection of upper wood from a tree or use of a juvenile individual. Additionally, high density of knots in wood may indicate a growth environment with a low basal area; perhaps indicative of a forest in a regenerative stage post-logging, a tree growing on a forest transition zone, or a tree growing in an open space such as an open field (e.g. pasture).

The use of spruce in ceiling planking provides additional conundrum in the interpretation of this vessel. Desmond (1919) indicates two types of spruce suitable for shipbuilding, black and white spruce. Both types are boreal and found only in the extreme northern United States. One other species of spruce available to shipwrights from the 1880s-1930s was red spruce cut from the Appalachian highlands of western North Carolina and eastern Tennessee (Lambert 1961). With the exception of Sitka spruce, other spruces appear identical and must undergo genetic testing for classification.

The Spring Break Wreck is exemplary of a vessel constructed during, or after, the last quarter of the nineteenth century. Double framing, as used with the Spring Break Wreck is a construction method typical of vessels built during the nineteenth century and following a general pattern of including horizontal fasteners, and leaving an air gap between rows of futtocks (Morris et al. 1995:125). Like the Seal Cove Wreck (Price et al. 2014), the Spring Break Wreck defies a nineteenth century trend (Morris et al. 1995) of favoring larger molded frame dimensions than sided. For Spring Break Wreck scantlings, see Meide, this volume. As mentioned, a lack of vessel repair or re-coppering indicates the vessel was not considerably old at the time of loss. Wood species used to construct the wreck indicate a reliance on dwindling hardwood resources and wood grain structure indicates a use of lower grade framing materials, including some juvenile trees.

Band sawmill cut marks on planking indicates a construction date no earlier than the 1880s. The vessel's builder was technically capable of machine cutting futtocks from flitches, but not able to saw tree trunks into flitches. This lack of connection with a common and critical need of a shipyard, custom sawmilling, may indicate that the builder was unaccustomed to shipbuilding. The curious selection of wood species too, points towards a certain degree of unfamiliarity with ship construction. Adze marks on ceiling timbers may further indicate an absence of custom sawmilling.

Paired beech and white pine is a method of framing yet encountered by the authors. Only one historic vessel has been identified with beech as a framing element. The Rose Hill shipwreck near Wilmington, North Carolina (Newsom 1988) intermixed beech with wood from the white oak (*Quercus* sp.) group in its futtocks. Based on construction elements, wood types, and artifactual evidence, the vessel was thought to have been a New England-built sloop outfitted for southern waters (Wilde-Ramsing et al. 1992). Perhaps the Spring Break Wreck too, was Yankee-built. Further analysis of the spruce ceiling timbers is in order. If the spruce proves to be an arboreal variety, such as white spruce (*Picea glauca*) or black spruce (*Picea marinana*), a northern build is likely. However, if red spruce (*Picea rubens*) is identified, there is a possibility for construction along the mid-Atlantic, possibly coastal North Carolina. This location would be the one place in North America close to the overlap of all identified species, and adjacent to a large timbering of red spruce during the late nineteenth century.

Wood selection and processing for the Spring Break Wreck vessel is a central node of study for this site. Mixing beech and white pine for framing introduces inherent weaknesses in fastener holding. Selecting woods susceptible to wet rot in lower structural components of a vessel further indicates a shipbuilder either ignorant of wood properties or an exigent circumstance during which these properties were overlooked. Such a circumstance might be during war, where good shipbuilding materials were unavailable, or during a period of economic boom where the need to build a vessel for immediate use outstripped the need for durability. Such a vessel would be classed under the American Lloyd's system as A1S, and only worthy of carrying the classification for seven years (Meyer and Salter 1883:ix). The substitution of beech and white pine for white oak points to a shipbuilding locale stripped of timber resources. Finally, the selection of juvenile white oak for treenails and juvenile beech for framing further indicate stress on local supplies of shipbuilding materials.

Conclusion

The Spring Break Wreck provides commentary on American shipbuilding during the terminal nineteenth century and early twentieth century. Overexploitation of wood resources throughout the United States left some craftsmen without quality building materials. Nonetheless, lack of quality materials failed to thwart the attempts of this builder. The Spring Break Wreck demonstrates a determination in building that speaks to a region in the periphery of modern shipbuilding. Failing to follow the futtock shape-trend identified by Morris et al. (1995) may indicate local, or vernacular, influence. Similarly, a lack of coaked futtock ends demonstrates a departure with late-nineteenth century shipbuilding vogue. Coaking was introduced as a method of preventing timber butt joints from shifting and utilizes a peg seated into each timber butt to maintain alignment.

Abuse of ecological systems resulted in anthropogenic problems such as this poorly built vessel. Conditions for its sailors and passengers were necessarily more dangerous; the ship was not meant to last and may have come apart under sail. In such a case, human interaction with an environment may have precipitated lethal consequences. Worked wood carries with it signatures of technology and environmental health – never tell your secrets to a tree. Secrets contained within Spring Break Wreck wood indicate poor environmental management in the form of depleted quality shipbuilding materials and wood harvested during a race to mow down mature southern pine forests.

These assertions, albeit tentative, offer a critique of nineteenth century consumerism and its attendant environmental impacts. The get-in and get-out mentality of nineteenth century logging drove American shipping by providing raw materials for shipbuilding and simultaneously necessitated the construction of great fleets to transport lumber. Many of these schooners, barks, and barkentines were built in professional shipyards, including foreign yards, as evident by the sample of lumber carriers wrecked at Dog Island, Florida during the hurricane of 1899 (Meide et al. 2001). However, not all of the merchants and lumber carriers were professionally built. Perhaps the Spring Break Wreck vessel was a late-century bark or schooner built by an enterprise unfamiliar with shipbuilding but with the zeal and capital to build. Such a yard may have relied on copying an older, existing vessel. Thus, a mimic was constructed. Without knowledge of appropriate framing materials or availability thereof, frames were constructed that were inherently damned. Lloyd's registry allows for blending of frames in the 1880s but classified the type of build as only worthy of insuring for seven years from launching (Meyer and Salter 1883:ix). Hand hewing flitches and then sawing futtocks with a bandsaw shows some measure of capital investment in tools and power, but not a ship saw. The same too, could be said for fastening. Iron drift bolts and spikes were used wherever metal fastening was found. Copper sheathing on the wreck indicates mimicry of tradition but without the knowledge that copper sheathing destroys iron fastening. In 1883, American Lloyd's Registry classification for vessels stipulated specific techniques of iron fastening where copper sheathing was used. Iron spikes were to be countersunk one inch and plugging with pine was one such recommendation (Meyer and Salter 1883:xvii). Builders of the Spring Break Wreck eschewed those recommendations.

The Spring Break Wreck may remain elusive in its origins and purpose but the wreck's enigmatic composition provides intricate contradictions of old and new shipbuilding methods and of shipbuilding knowledge and shipbuilding ignorance. Wood analysis and processing marks, examined here, contribute valuable information on the terminal period of American wooden shipbuilding and regional variation. The selection of materials and inability of custom sawmilling exhibits an amount of disconnect with the professional shipbuilding world; perhaps indicative of peripheral shipbuilding in technical skill and geography. Without closely analyzing the site's wooden fabric these subtleties may have gone unnoticed and this wreck relegated to the heap of mute nineteenth century shipwrecks.

Acknowledgements

The authors wish to thank the Florida Public Archaeology Network (FPAN), SEARCH Inc., the Guana Tolomato Matanzas National Estuarine Research Reserve (GTM-NERR), John Valdes & Associates, Construction Debris Removal, Inc., Sunbelt Rentals, and numerous volunteers who made recordation and relocation of this vessel possible.

References

AMERICAN FOREST PRODUCTS LABORATORY (AFPL)
2010   Wood Handbook: Wood as an Engineering Material. United States Department of Agriculture. Madison, Wisconsin. Also available at <https://www.fpl.fs.fed.us/documnts/fplgtr/fpl_gtr190.pdf>.

CLEMENT, WINSTON WALLACE
2014   Standardization in the Lumber Industry; Trade Journals, Builders Guides and the American Home. Master's Thesis. Graduate Program in Historic Preservation. University of Pennsylvania. Philadelphia, Pennsylvania.

CURTIS, WILLIAM HENRY
2009   *The Elements of Wood Ship Construction.* Reprint of 1919 edition. Algrove Publishing. Almonte, Ontario.

DESMOND, CHARLES
1919   *Wooden Shipbuilding.* Rudder Publishing Company, New York.

GOODWIN, PETER
1997   "The Influence of Iron in Ship Construction: 1660 to 1830". Paper presented at the Maritime Park Association annual conference. 8 July. San Francisco Maritime Park, California.

HARLEY, C. K.
1973   "On the Persistence of Old Techniques: The Case of North American Wooden Shipbuilding". *The Journal of Economic History.* Vol 33, No. 2. Cambridge University Press. Cambridge, United Kingdom.

HOLLAND, A. J.
1985   *Buckler's Hard: A Rural Shipbuilding Center.* Kenneth Mason Publications, Emsworth, United Kingdom.

HOYT, HOMER
1919   *Prices of Building Materials.* Government Printing Office, Washington, D.C.

IAWA COMMITTEE
1989   IAWA list of microscopic features for hardwood identification, with an appendix on non-anatomical information, Wheeler, E.A., P. Baas, and P.E. Gasson, eds. IAWA Bulletin n.s. 10(3):219-332.

IAWA COMMITTEE
2004   IAWA list of microscopic features for softwood identification, H.G. Richter, D. Grosser, I. Heinz, and P.E. Gasson, eds. IAWA Journal 25(1):1-70.

INSIDEWOOD
2004-onwards. Published on the Internet. <http://insidewood.lib.ncsu.edu/search> Accessed 15 November 2018.

LAMBERT, ROBERT S.
1961   "Logging in the Great Smokies, 1880-1930" *Tennessee Historical Quarterly* 20(4): 350-363.

MCALISTER, ROBERT
2013   *The Lumber Boom of Coastal South Carolina; Nineteenth-Century Shipbuilding and the Devastation of Lowcountry Virgin Forests.* The History Press, Charleston, South Carolina.

MEIDE, CHUCK, JAMES A MCCLEAN, AND EDWARD WISER
2001   *Dog Island Shipwreck Survey 1999: Report of Historical and Archaeological Investigations.* Edited by Michael K. Faught, Jennifer McKinnon, William T. Hoffman, and Joe M. Latvis. Program in Underwater Archaeology, Florida State University. Tallahassee, Florida.

MEYER, H. F. A. AND C. FREDERICK SALTER
1883   American Lloyd's Register of American and Foreign Shipping. Charles Vogt. New York, New York. Online manuscript https://research.mysticseaport.org/item/l0237571883/9/

MORRIS, JOHN W. III, GORDON P. WATTS, JR., AND MARIANNE FRANKLIN
1995   "The Comparative Analysis of 18th Century Vessel Remains in the Archaeological Record: A Synthesized Theory of Framing Evolution". In *Underwater Archaeology Proceedings from the Society for Historical Archaeology Conference,* ed. by Paul Forsythe Johnston, 125–133. Society for Historical Archaeology, Washington, DC.

NEWSOM, LEE A.
1988   Wood identification of Rose Hill shipwreck timber samples. Ms. on file, The Florida State Museum, University of Florida, Gainesville, Florida.

PANSHIN, A.J., AND C. DE ZEEUW.
1980.   *Textbook of Wood Technnology: Structure, Identification, Properties, and Uses of the Commercial Woods of the United States and Canada*, Fourth Edition. McGraw-Hill Book Company, New York.

PRESCOTT, D. CLINTON
1910   *The Evolution of Modern Band Saw Mills for Sawing Logs*. The Prescott Company, Menominee, Michigan.

PRICE, FRANKLIN, STEPHEN DILK, AND BAYLUS BROOKS JR.
2014   "The Seal Cove Shipwreck Project: Investigating an Historic Wooden Vessel on Mount Desert Island, Maine". *In Northeast Historic Archaeology*. 43(7).

SLOANE, ERIC
1965   *A Reverence for Wood*. Funk and Wagnalls, New York. Reprinted 2004 by Dover Publications. Mineola, New York.

THIESEN, WILLIAM H.
2006   *Industrializing American Shipbuilding: The Transformation of Ship Design and Construction, 1820-1920*. University Press of Florida, Gainesville, Florida.

UNITED STATES NAVY BUREAU OF SHIPS (BUSHIPS)
1983   *Wood: A Manual for its Use as a Shipbuilding Material*. Vol. 1. Reprint of 1957 revision. Teaparty Books, Kingston, Massachusetts.

WILDE-RAMSING, MARK U., WILSON ANGLEY, RICHARD W. LAWRENCE, AND GEOFFREY J. SCOFIELD
1992   *The Rose Hill Wreck: Historical and Archaeological Investigations of an Eighteenth Century Vessel at a Colonial River Landing near Wilmington, North Carolina*. Underwater Archaeology Branch, Division of Archives and History. North Carolina Department of Cultural Resources, Kure Beach, North Carolina.

WHEELER, E.A.
2011   InsideWood - a web resource for hardwood anatomy. *IAWA Journal* 32 (2): 199-211.

• • • • • • • • • • • • • • • •

P. Brendan Burke
St. Augustine Lighthouse & Maritime Museum
81 Lighthouse Avenue
St. Augustine, Florida 32080
904-829-0745 x202
bburke@staugustinelighthouse.org

Lee Newsom
Flagler College
74 King Street
St. Augustine, Florida 32084
800-304-4208
lnewsom@flagler.edu

Happy Anniversary! We Didn't Get You A Card but We Found a Lot of Ship: Revisiting the Anniversary Wreck.

Silvana Kreines, Chuck Meide, Megan Bebee

In July 2015, during the city's 450th anniversary celebration, a buried shipwreck was discovered off St. Augustine, Florida by the St. Augustine Lighthouse Archaeological Maritime Program, or LAMP. Test excavations in 2015-2016 revealed a remarkable amount of material culture, including barrels, cauldrons, pewter plates, shoe buckles, cut stone, and a variety of glass and ceramics. These artifacts tentatively dated the vessel to 1750-1800 and suggested its nationality was likely British, but possibly Spanish or American. The abundance, spatial distribution, and stylistic uniformity of the artifacts suggest they were cargo items, leading to the working hypothesis that this was a merchant ship run aground while trying to enter St. Augustine's notorious inlet. In the summer of 2018, with a team of field school students and volunteer divers, LAMP returned to the site to conduct further excavation. This paper summarizes the results of the 2018 season on this shipwreck.

St. Augustine's Inlet, Shipwrecks, and the Discovery of the Anniversary Wreck

"It has become so common at St. Augustine to see ships aground on this bar...disasters of the sort have almost ceased to arouse sympathy or wonder" (Schoepf 1788:227). This quote is from the German botanist and physician Dr. Johann Schoepf, who traveled to America in 1777 to work as Chief Surgeon for the British Army. After the Revolutionary War ended, he traveled America, including a visit to St. Augustine where he witnessed numerous shipwrecks in the port's notorious inlet. These ship losses were so striking that he discussed them extensively in his book Travels in the Confederation upon returning to Europe in 1784. He continued,

> *The sand bar before St. Augustine is unquestionably the most dangerous because [it is] the shallowest and at the same time exposed to the total force of the ocean playing upon it... It is indeed a fearful thing to hear the wild tumult of these breaking seas and to behold them on all sides foaming and tossing... (Schoepf 1788:227).*

It is believed that the inlet has shifted drastically over the years. Conch Island, a peninsula jutting from Anastasia Island off the coast of St. Augustine, did not exist at the time. It formed from the existing shoals (North Breakers) in the 1940s as a result of dredging operations in the modern inlet. The shoals or sand bars off this coast are what made the city home to one of the most dangerous inlets in the continental United States. They would shift away or build up on a continual basis, causing shipwrecks as often as twice a month (Schoepf 1788:249). With such frequency, local residents were used to shipwrecks and kept a regular look out, sounding an alarm when an approaching ship was sighted to warn that a rescue might be necessary. Keeping watch for shipwrecks and launching rescue attempts would become among the official duties of the St. Augustine Lighthouse Keeper.

The Anniversary Wreck was discovered in 2015 by LAMP archaeologists during a remote sensing survey. LAMP serves as the research arm of the St. Augustine Lighthouse & Maritime Museum. The magnetic target delineated in the survey was designated "Silver Surfer." It was subsequently tested by divers using a hydraulic probe, resulting in a series of hard returns suggesting a large concentration of possible wreckage within a five by seven-meter area. Two adjacent 1 x 1 meter test units were excavated, revealing a wide array of artifacts. Upon confirmation that this was, indeed, an historic shipwreck, the site was named "Anniversary Wreck" in honor of the 450th anniversary of St. Augustine's founding which was celebrated that year. Anniversary Wreck is situated well to the north of St. Augustine's former channel, around which all other St. Augustine shipwrecks dating to the 18th and 19th centuries have been found, to date. The anomalous location of this shipwreck places it well inside of St. Augustine's notorious North Breakers, suggesting the captain of this vessel was considerably off course, perhaps with no control over his vessel at the time of wrecking. It is also possible that the captain was ignorant of the local environment and made an unfortunate attempt to sail through one of the lesser inlets sometimes used by fishing boats but inadequate for larger ships.

Initial test excavations revealed a remarkable amount of material culture, including cauldrons, barrels, pewter plates, unidentified concreted objects, and a variety of glass and ceramics (Meide 2017:12-14). The density of artifacts encountered on the Anniversary Wreck during this test excavation surpassed that of the Storm Wreck, excavated between 2010 and 2015 (Veilleux and Meide 2016). Cauldrons and casks are among the largest and most frequently unearthed artifacts on the wreck, to date. Around 30 cauldrons have been found on site, often nested together for more efficient stowage. Their numbers and positions suggest they were a cargo item intended for the markets of St. Augustine, rather than personal possessions. The cauldrons can be roughly dated to between 1740 and 1780 (Meide 2017:15-16). The wooden components of the casks are mostly or fully deteriorated, leaving cask-shaped concretions, suggesting contents of perhaps iron hardware. Date ranges from the cauldrons, pewterware, and ceramics initially suggested a date range of 1750-1800.

Summary of 2016 Fieldwork

Field work on the Anniversary Wreck during the 2016 season (Meide 2017) focused first on further delineation of the site with remote sensing and then continued excavation around the original 2015 test units. Carried out over 22 days of diving between July and September, excavators logged a total of 342 dives for a cumulative bottom time of 276 hours, 40 minutes. Before sediment disturbance commenced, a refinement survey of the site using magnetometer and side scan sonar was conducted with lane spacing of 5 m (16.24 ft.). A total of ten new excavation units were placed. Once Units 1 and 2 were re-exposed, grids for Units 3-8 were established and sediment removal by suction dredge continued until a 2 m x 4 m area was exposed for recording. The methodology used for investigations at this site is summarized in Meide 2017 (12-14). Nine days of excavation were completed in 2016 before enough sand had been removed to achieve an angle of repose in the sidewalls to prevent continual infill. Once Units 1-8 were stable, the area was recorded by hand drawing and digital video.

With the initial excavation area recorded, four more test units (9-12) were established along the western border. Only two days of excavation were completed before a protracted period of bad weather suspended field activities on site. During that limited time, divers were able to expose, record, and recover the artifacts in Unit 10, but were unable to complete Units 9, 11, and 12. The 3 x 4 m area tested in 2016 exposed 8 concreted barrels, 21 ceramics (primarily brown stoneware), 7 pewter plates, 12 brass shoe buckle frames, 3 blocks of dressed stone, and 28 cast-iron cauldrons. Preliminary analyses of the 2016 field season are consistent with the hypothesis that this ship may have been a merchant vessel laden with cargo which wrecked while attempting to enter the port of St. Augustine sometime between 1750 and 1800 (Meide 2017).

Other 2016 activities in the vicinity of the Anniversary Wreck included the testing of a magnetic anomaly that was located only 90 m away, which was believed to possibly represent another component of the shipwreck. No buried remains were detected, however, despite 124 hydraulic probe tests.

Summary of 2017 Fieldwork

Fieldwork on the Anniversary Wreck during the 2017 season was dedicated to exploring the areas to the west of the original units and those excavated in 2016. Diving was carried out over 21 days in June, July, and August. A total of 365 dives were logged, totaling just one minute shy of 281 hours underwater. Once Units 1 through 12 were re-exposed, grids for Units 13-18 were established and excavation continued in these new units. Ten days of excavation were completed to expose the buried remains. However, due to extremely poor visibility and inclement weather, minimal documentation and artifact recovery took place, as sediment accretion reburied excavated areas when divers could not be present on the site.

Five test units (13-17) were established along the western boarder of the previous units, as well as one test unit (18) to the north of Unit 12. Although ten days of excavation were completed, minimal documentation was accomplished for the reasons given above. Only Unit 15 was fully mapped and added to the site plan. No scaled drawings were completed for Units 9, 11, 12, 13, 14, 16, 17, and 18. Sketches, not to exact scale, for Units 11 and 12 were made from observing the units and immediately illustrating them on the boat. These sketches were added to the site plan as a placeholder until scaled recordings can be completed. The remaining units appear blank on the site plan. Work continued in these units during the 2018 field season.

The new units covering a 1 x 5 m area exposed 1 cauldron, 1 concreted barrel, 1 full pewter plate and the rim of a second pewter plate, 1 brass shoe buckle, three pieces of ceramics (two pieces of brick and/or tile, and one brown stoneware), an additional block of dressed stone, as well as lead shot and glass fragments (Meide 2017:24-26). A total of forty-three sediment samples were also taken at the start and end of every dive for all of the units (Meide 2017:26-27). These sediments samples came from Units 2, 10, 11, 12, 13, 14, 15, 16, 17, and 18. A series of core samples were collected to better understand site stratigraphy. These consisted of simple clear, plastic tubes of about one meter in length and 2.5 cm in diameter, hammered by the divers into the sea bottom, and then capped as they were withdrawn. Micro-layers of stratigraphy were discernable and recorded upon initial inspection. The samples have been provided to Dr. Lee Newsom of Flagler College for a more thorough microscopic analysis. Core samples were taken from the SW corner of Unit 16, and one from the SW corner of Unit 14. Nothing recovered in this season challenged the working hypothesis concerning the vessel's function, while the presence of creamware narrowed down the suspected date range slightly, to 1762-1800 (Meide 2017:29).

Summary of 2018 Fieldwork

Zero visibility and repeated stretches of foul weather disallowed significant excavation progress during the 2018 field season. Only 17 days of diving could be completed on the site, totaling 238 dives for 163 hours, 58 minutes of bottom time. Fieldwork on the Anniversary Wreck during the 2018 season was dedicated to exploring the areas originally exposed during previous field seasons. Eight grid units were placed and ten days of excavation in Units 11, 12, 14, 15, 16, and 17. Although two new units, Units 19 and 20, were established to the west of Units 15 and 16, inclement weather prohibited exposure of any cultural remains in those new units.

Wreckage was exposed in Units 11, 12, 15, and 16. Scaled drawings were completed for Units 11, 12, and 16. Unit 15 was recorded in 2017 and artifacts previously documented were recovered in 2018. At the time of this writing, the newly recorded units are being added to the overall site plan.

The recorded units encompassed a 2 x 2 m area and included one cauldron, one concreted barrel, and a handful of large and unidentified concretions that were not collected. Recovered artifacts include fifteen concretions, one intact pewter plate, one block of dressed stone, two ceramic sherds (including a datable feather edge creamware plate rim), two door knobs, several clothing irons, one gun flint, one key, one key escutcheon, lead shot, brass tacks, seeds, nuts, and wood fragments. Thirty-four sediment samples were also collected, one at the start and end of every dredge team per unit. These samples came from Units 11, 12, 14, 15, 16, 17, 19, and 20. Preliminary analysis of these artifacts has narrowed down the date range only slightly, to sometime between 1765 and 1800 (Meide 2018). This is based on the origin of featheredged creamware as 1765 as reported by Noël Hume (2001:125).

In addition to the concretions recovered in 2018, concretions collected in previous seasons were x-rayed in 2018. These x-rays revealed more artifacts including lead shot, tacks, shoe buckles, pewter plates, key escutcheons, seeds and fruit pits, clothing irons and padlocks. These artifacts from 2018, some of which have been analyzed in concretion by radiography, are summarized in the remainder of this paper.

Padlocks

In total, five padlocks were recovered from Anniversary Wreck during the 2016-2018 field seasons. All but one of these padlocks appear to be stylistically similar, resembling a purse or bag style. This style came into existence in the late seventeenth century but is commonly associated with eighteenth century North American English contexts (Karklins 2000:79-80). Three of the four similar padlocks were recovered from the northeastern corner of Unit 8 at a depth of 130 cm below datum; the fourth was recovered about a meter north in Unit 2 at a depth of 150 cm below datum. The fifth, and only stylistically distinct padlock, was recovered from Unit 7, which boarders Unit 8 to the east, from a depth between 50-140 centimeters below datum. This outlier appears to be a small ball padlock.

Figure 1a shows Field Specimen 16SS-045.01, a concretion with a single padlock of the purse/bag style, which has much of its inner mechanisms intact. This padlock is taller than it is wide and has a rounded shape with low shoulders. While early examples of this style would have been small and broader than they were tall, their shape began to evolve at the turn of the century, becoming taller, more pointed, and larger (Noël Hume 1969:250-251). The overall shape and size of this artifact suggests an eighteenth-century date.

Clothing Irons

Four concretions containing clothing irons were recovered during the 2016-2018 field seasons. Three of these Field Specimens (16SS-069.01, 18SS-388.01,

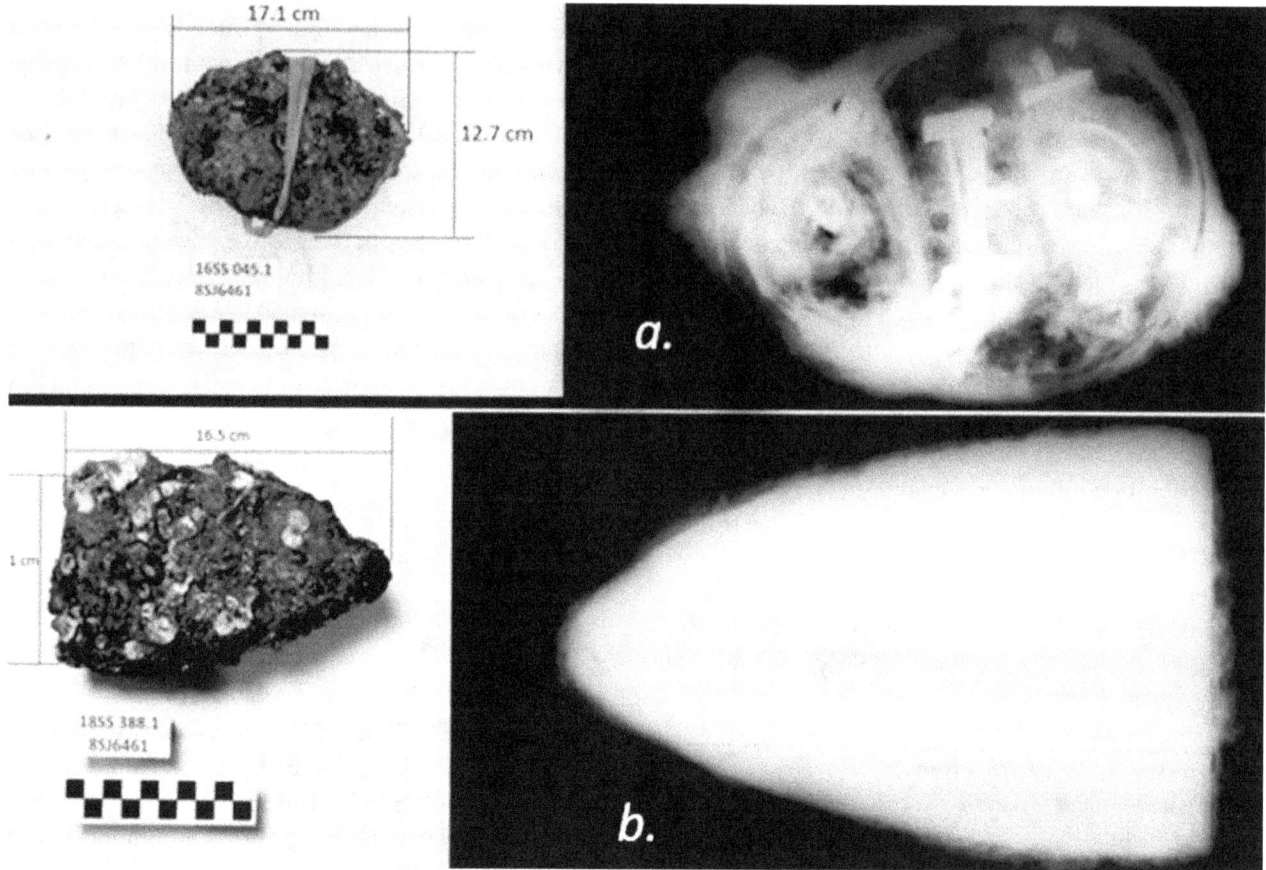

FIGURE 1: Concretions and their X-ray images taken by Starr Cox of (a) an iron padlock and (b) a clothing iron.

18SS-392.1) appear to contain one iron each (Figure 1b). The fourth concretion (18SS-389.01) is larger and heavy, and appears to the naked eye to be a conglomerate made up of multiple irons. X-ray imaging was somewhat nebulous, as the x-rays could not fully penetrate the mass, and revealed only one definite iron, along with lead shot and brass tacks.

All of the clothing irons that can be identified in the x-ray images appear to be of similar design and dimensions. The imagery suggests that these are flat or sad irons. The term "sad" here is actually defined as heavy or solid (Smith 1996). Flat irons have been used since the medieval period in Europe, consisting of a solid, triangular metal base with a metal or detachable wooden handle (ibid). This simple design, along with the box iron, which was hollow with a rear door for inserting hot iron inserts or coals, was popular in Colonial America. Flat or sad irons could weigh from five to nine pounds with some examples weighing more (Smith 1996). The heavy weight of these objects supports the supposition that these are flat rather than box irons. These simple irons were placed in the hearth and warmed to the proper temperature. If too hot, they would scorch the clothing. Women in the household usually used at least two of these types of irons in tandem in order to have one heating while the other was in use. These irons are similar in form to those found on the 1782 Storm Wreck (McCarron 2016:172).

Field Specimens 18SS-0388.1 and 18SS-389.1 were both recovered from Unit 11. Field Specimen 18SS-392.1 was from a diagonally adjacent unit, 16, as was 16SS-69.1, in Unit 3. Though it would be typical for pairs of irons to be in contextual association with each other, the provenience and numbers of these irons suggests that they were being transported as cargo rather than personal items.

Peach Pits

A total of 76 different seeds or similar organic remains were found on site, ranging from unidentified seeds to a mangrove propagule (pod), nut shells, olive pits and peach pits. In many cases it can be difficult to determine if such organic remains are invasive materials to the shipwreck or were part of the vessel's cargo. One exception is peach pits. Significant quantities of peach pits have

FIGURE 2: Two of the eleven peach pits found in Unit 15.

been found on the site (Figure 2). To date, eleven peach pits have been recovered, all from the dredge spoil. All but one was found in Unit 15. Due to the quantity and spatial distribution of the peach pits, it is believed that they were part of the vessel's cargo and not intrusive to the site.

Peaches were introduced into Colonial North America by the Spanish monks who traveled to and lived in St. Augustine, Florida with Pedro Menendez de Aviles in the 1560s. The peach became a common crop among the colonists in St. Augustine, as well as the surrounding native communities (Ruhl 2018). By the late 1500s, peaches had been introduced to St. Simons Island and Cumberland Island, Georgia by Franciscan monks (Hale Groves 2012). As missionaries traveled north and native trade occurred, the peach plant migrated north. By 1607, peaches were widespread in the mid-Atlantic region (Okie 2017). The Cherokee Indians were documented to have been planting peaches in Georgia and the Carolinas in the 1700s (Hale Groves 2012). Peach pits have been discovered on other shipwreck sites as well, including the Soldier Key Wreck (early 1700s), the Tortugas Wreck (late 1600s), and the Emanuel Point Wrecks (1559).

Peaches were in season in Florida from mid-April to early May and in Georgia and South Carolina from mid-May to late August. This could suggest a seasonal range indicating when the ship may have wrecked, though it is always possible that the peaches could have been preserved and were being shipped in the off-season. It should also be noted that St. Augustine's most important trading partners during this period were the ports of Savannah and Charleston, both from a region where the commercial production of peaches thrived. This is the kind of cargo expected on an incoming merchant vessel (as opposed to oranges, which would have been exported from Florida to Georgia and the Carolinas).

Pewter Plates

Seven pewter plates were encountered in 2016, four of which were recovered (16SS-19.1, 16SS-84.1, 16SS-87.1, 16SS-90.1). An additional plate and a separate rim section were recovered the following year (17SS-234.1, 17SS235.1) (Meide 2017:25). In 2018, concretion 18SS-387.1 was recovered, which included a partially exposed plate (Figure 3a).

The legal standard for eighteenth century fine pewter consisted of 94 percent tin with a 6% mixture of other metals such as lead, copper, and antimony (Carlson 1977:65). The plate recovered in 2018 remains in relatively good condition and, like most of the others, appears to be a shallow-welled, single rim pewter plate. Based on the size and shape, this appears to be a trencher, intended for use by a single individual rather than as a serving platter. Pewter was a popular choice for tableware from the medieval period through the colonial period because it was relatively inexpensive (Gardener 1894: 629); however, it fell in and out of favor in the early 19th century. The single-reeded and smooth-edged rim styles present on the Anniversary Wreck plates provide a date range of ca. 1720-1800 (Neumann 1984:276-277).

Tacks

A great quantity of tacks have been x-ray imaged in 23 separate concretions recovered from the shipwreck. These concretions were collected from various units and depths which suggests that if they were a cargo item, they have been widely scattered by site formation processes. All of the tacks appear to be square-shanked with circular, concavo-convex heads around a half-inch in diameter. This style of tack originates in the seventeenth century; the earliest examples were typically up to one inch in diameter (Noël Hume 1969:227-228). These tacks were used for upholstery, either to decorate or anchor the leather on furniture, and likewise would have been used on leather-bound trunks or luggage. Their head size suggests a later date since brass tacks decreased in size during the eighteenth-century (Noël Hume 1969:228).

Shoe Buckles

One of the recently x-rayed concretions featured one shoe buckle and one fastener hollow (Figure 3b). A total

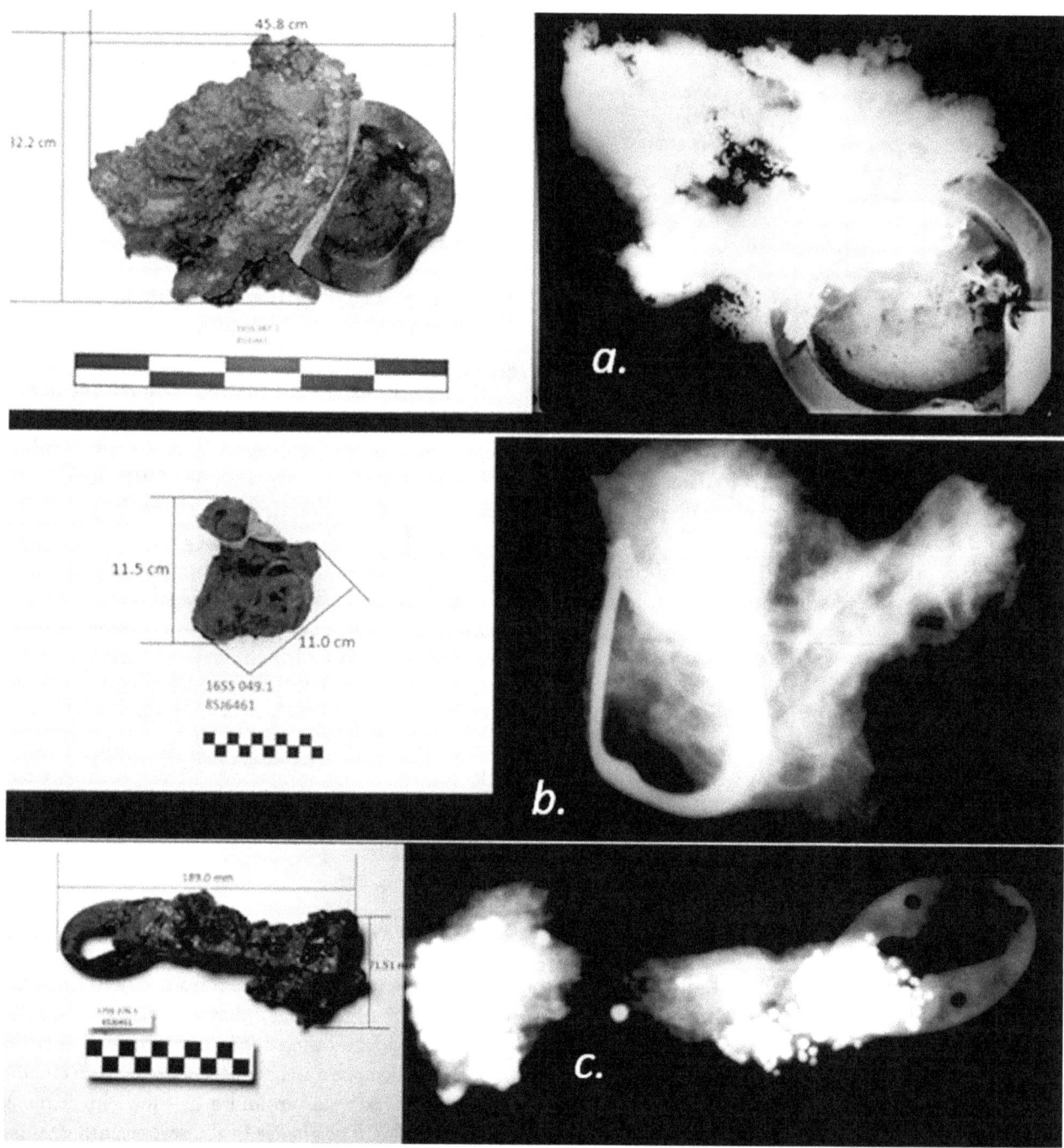

FIGURE 3: Concretions and their X-ray images taken by Starr Cox of (a) one protruding pewter plate alongside brass tacks and Rupert lead shot, (b) one brass shoe buckle and one fastener hollow, and (c) a keyhole alongside Rupert lead shot.

of thirteen whole and partial buckle frames have been recovered from the Anniversary Wreck to date. All but one of the stylistically similar frames were located in a relatively confined area, suggesting they were cargo rather than personal items. This is in contrast to those found on the Storm Wreck, a refugee vessel with many passengers, where shoe buckles varied in material, style, and provenience (Brendel 2016:191).

This type of brass shoe buckle was common from the first half of the 16th century, though they have not usually been found on American sites until the early 1700s. Their use was revived just before the 1690s and remained fashionable until after the French Revolution in 1789 when they became unpopular. They are very rarely found after 1815 on American sites (Noël Hume 1969:86). All buckles found on the Anniversary Wreck site lack any decoration. The frames are a simple shape that more closely resembles an oval than a rectangle due to its rounded edges. The frames have been curved to fit the top of the foot, are flat in cross-section, and feature a Type 1 pin terminal (White 2005:34).

Keyhole Escutcheons, Key, and Tap

Figure 3c shows a small concretion, Field Specimen 17SS-276.1, which features an exposed keyhole escutcheon. This key plate is simple and is devoid of any decoration, suggesting that it dates to during or after the 1760s, when larger, decorative keyhole escutcheons began to go out of style (Noël Hume 1969:231). A similar keyhole escutcheon can be seen in x-ray imagery of another concretion (18SS-375.1), along with a key. The key may not have been intended for the associated keyhole plate, however, as it appears to be a keg tap key. A brass keg tap was recovered in 2018, embedded in concretion 18SS-394.1, and is partially visible in x-ray imagery.

Door Knobs

Two door knobs were found during the 2018 excavations. One is embedded in concretion 18SS-377.1 from Unit 1 and has not been measured, though x-ray imagery suggests it is similar in form and size to the second specimen (18SS-383.1), which was discovered loose in Unit 15. The exposed knob is brass, oval in shape, and may have part of its spindle in the back of its neck (Figure 4).

Door knobs in the eighteenth century ranged in shape and make. The early eighteenth century, when door knobs first gained popularity, saw a spherical brass knob. Door knobs were more ovular in the mid-eighteenth century. By the end of the century, door knobs had become flat and circular, a form which continued well into the nineteenth century (Noël Hume 1969:246). This suggests the Anniversary Wreck door knobs date to the middle of the 18th century. It has not yet been determined if these knobs were part of the ship's cabin hardware or if they were a cargo item. If more are found, it is more likely that they were intended for the St. Augustine market.

Conclusion

Data gleaned from this shipwreck continues to grow after three seasons of formal excavation, leading to an evolving and better understanding of this shipwreck. The Anniversary Wreck features a dense deposit of material culture buried more than a meter below the sand, and further excavation promises more material. The great quantity of cauldrons, barrels, plates, and buckles, and their stylistic homogeneity, indicate that this ship was a merchant vessel loaded with cargo, attempting to enter St. Augustine when it ran aground and broke up on the bar. All of these objects could be seaborne imports that would have been valued in St. Augustine's markets. Other hardware items discovered in the 2018 season, including tacks, door knobs, locking mechanisms, and the tap, could also be cargo items.

It appears that most of the diagnostic artifacts are of British origin. This does not necessarily mean that the ship was British, as an early American vessel might be plying similar wares, or a Spanish vessel might have been trading illegally with British colonies (Harman 1969; Deagan 2007). But a strong possibility remains that this ship was English. Many of the artifacts are datable, and suggest with a good degree of certainty a date range of 1765-1800. Much of this analysis is in a preliminary stage, and the date range can be further narrowed with continued excavation and analysis. This three and a half decade span was a period of cultural transformations in St. Augustine, as it shifted from Spanish to British and then back to Spanish control.

It is evident that this shipwreck site has significant archaeological potential. This is the only colonial-era merchant vessel that has been discovered in the waters off America's oldest port, and it features a wealth of material culture. Further excavation will lead to a greater understanding of the nature and extent of the wreckage and its cultural and temporal origins. Once the ship's date and nationality are refined, then archaeologists can bring into focus the cargo items and better understand

FIGURE 4: One of the two door knobs found in Anniversary Wreck's assemblage.

this ship's role in the emerging global capitalist system. The continued archaeology of the Anniversary Wreck will allow for more meaningful questions and an informed exploration of 18th-century consumerism and its reflection of the desires and needs of St. Augustine's colonial population during a time of sociocultural change.

Acknowledgments

The 2015-2018 excavations were funded by field school fees and with grants from the Bureau of Historic Preservation, Division of Historical Resources, Florida Department of State through the Florida Historical Commission. Dave Howe, Mike Potter and Kevin Carrigan have provided research vessels, and the Hutcherson family dock space, to support our research. The project's success ultimately lies with the team of LAMP and St. Augustine Lighthouse & Maritime Museum staff, students, and volunteers who have given time, talent, and passion to this shipwreck. There are too many to name here, but thanks to everyone.

References

BRENDEL, HUNTER
2016   Personal Items from the Storm Wreck. In *ACUA Underwater Archaeology Proceedings 2016*, edited by Paul F. Johnston, pp. 187-193, Washington, D.C.

CARLSON, JANICE H
1977   Analysis of British and American Pewter by X-Ray Fluorescence Spectroscopy, *Winterthur portfolio*. Vol. 12. pp. 65-85. The University of Chicago Press.

DEAGAN, KATHLEEN
2007   Eliciting Contraband through Archaeology: Illicit Trade in Eighteenth-Century St. Augustine. *Historical Archaeology* 41(4):98-116.

GARDENER, J. STARKIE
1894   *Journal of the Society of the Arts* Vol. 42. No. 2167 June 1, 1894 Royal society for the Encouragement of Arts, Manufactures and Commerce. London. pp 627-648

HALE GROVES
2012   *Georgia Peaches Have a Rich History* https://www.halegroves.com/blog/georgia-peaches-have-a-rich-history/

HARMAN, JOYCE ELIZABETH
1969   *Trade and Privateering in Spanish Florida* 1732-1763. St. Augustine Historical Society, St. Augustine, Florida.

KARKLINS, KARLIS (EDITOR)
2000   "Historic Door Hardware" *Studies in Material Culture Research*, Society for Historical Archaeology pp. 79-80

MCCARRON, CHRISTOPHER
2016   Household Artifacts from the Storm Wreck. In *ACUA Underwater Archaeology Proceedings 2016*, edited by Paul F. Johnston, pp. 169-176, Washington, D.C.

MEIDE, CHUCK
2017   The Investigation of the Anniversary Wreck, a Colonial Period Shipwreck off St. Augustine, Florida: Results of the First Excavation Season. In *ACUA Underwater Archaeology Proceedings 2017*, edited by John Albertson and Frederick H. Hanselmann. Advisory Council on Underwater Archaeology, Forth Worth, TX.

MEIDE, CHUCK
2018   The Investigation of the Anniversary Wreck, a Colonial Period Shipwreck Lost off St. Augustine, Florida: Results of the 2017 Excavation Season. In *ACUA Underwater Archaeology Proceedings 2018*, edited by Matthew E. Keith and Amanda M. Evans, pp. 21-29. Advisory Council on Underwater Archaeology, New Orleans, LA.

NEUMANN, GEORGE C.
1984   *Early American Antique Country Furnishings: Northeastern America*, 1650-1800. McGraw-Hill, New York.

NOËL HUME, IVOR
1969   *A Guide to Artifacts of Colonial America* pp. 250-251 Chipstone Foundation, Milwaukee, WI.

2001   *If These Pots Could Talk: Collecting 2,000 Years of British Household Pottery*. Chipstone Foundation, Milwaukee, WI.

OKIE, WILLIAM THOMAS
2017   *The Fuzzy History of the Georgia Peach* <https://www.smithsonianmag.com/history/fuzzy-history-georgia-peach-180964490/>.

RUHL, DONNA
2018   *Object 85: Peach pits* (Florida Museum of Natural History.) <https://www.floridamuseum.ufl.edu/100years/peach-pits/>.

SMITH, LESLIE
1996   The Sad Iron(y) of These Collectibles. Chicago Tribune <https://www.chicagotribune.com/news/ct-xpm-1996-08-11-9608110129-story.html>.

SCHOEPF, JOHANN DAVID
1911 [1788]   *Travels in the Confederation* (1783-1784). William J. Campbell, Philadelphia.

VEILLEUX, CAROLANE AND CHUCK MEIDE
2016   The Archaeological Investigation of the Storm Wreck, a Wartime Refugee Vessel Lost at St. Augustine, Florida, at the End of the Revolutionary War: Overview of the 2010-2015 Excavation Seasons. In *ACUA Underwater Archaeology Proceedings 2016*, edited by Paul F. Johnston, pp. 122-132, Washington, D.C.

WHITE, CAROLYN L.
2005   *American Artifacts of Personal Adornment,* 1680-1820: A Guide to Identification and Interpretation. AltaMira Press, Lanham, MD

. . . .

Silvana Kreines
LG2 Environmental Solutions
10475 Fortune Parkway
Jacksonville, FL 32256
Cell: (917) 757-2984
silvana.kreines@gmail.com

Chuck Meide
Lighthouse Archaeological Maritime Program (LAMP)
81 Lighthouse Avenue
St Augustine, FL 32080
Cell: (904) 838-9059
cmeide@staugustinelighthouse.org

Megan Bebee
LG2 Environmental Solutions
10475 Fortune Parkway
Jacksonville, FL 32256
Cell: (631) 258-4905
mbebee@lg2es.com

Heritage Monitoring Underwater: Launching the Submerged Heritage Monitoring Scouts Florida Program

Rachael Kangas, Jeffrey Moates, Brenda Altmeier, Sara Ayers-Rigsby

The Florida Public Archaeology Network's (FPAN) successful Heritage Monitoring Scout (HMS) Program, launched in 2016, was adapted for underwater sites as Submerged Heritage Monitoring Scout (SHMS) when FPAN partnered with Florida Keys National Marine Sanctuary (FKNMS) following Hurricane Irma in 2017. Lack of personnel, difficulty with routinely accessing sites, coupled with the "out of sight, out of mind" mentality make submerged historical sites vulnerable. This program teaches divers what submerged historical sites are, the importance of monitoring, and laws that protect underwater resources. Heritage Monitoring Scouts, both terrestrial and submerged, learn how they can effectively monitor sites with the ease of checking a box from their phone. Since its launch in 2018, the program has focused on established shipwreck trails, such as the FKNMS Shipwreck Trail. The program has great potential to contribute important data on submerged historical sites in Florida and the effects of climate change on these non-renewable resources.

Introduction

Submerged historical resources in Florida are at ever-increasing risk due to the impacts and complications of climate change. Many submerged historical resources have not been visited, lack proper documentation, and overall are under-studied. While threats to historical resources are steady and ongoing, major weather events such as storms, increase this process by potentially damaging sites and exposing sensitive artifacts. Lack of staff at federal and state agencies, difficulty with routinely accessing sites, coupled with the "out of sight, out of mind" mentality make submerged historical sites vulnerable to myriad threats.

After a number of significant changes to submerged historical resources in the Florida Keys National Marine Sanctuary (FKNMS) following Hurricane Irma in 2017, sanctuary staff recognized the necessity to engage the community to assist with reporting such changes. Documenting sites regularly helps researchers and managers better understand threats and illuminate effects on submerged historical resources. The Florida Public Archaeology Network (FPAN) and FKNMS adapted FPAN's terrestrial citizen science program, Heritage Monitoring Scouts (HMS) Florida, to empower divers to make important contributions by documenting change and monitoring shipwrecks in Florida waters. The submerged program uses the same platform and some of the same questions to gather data about site location, condition, and priority. The Submerged HMS (SHMS) Florida program is currently in its pilot stage, having trained several groups in the Florida Keys. SHMS has the potential to contribute significantly to the understanding of impacts of climate change on submerged historical resources as well as potential for the data collected to impact historical resource studies and our understanding of climate change.

Climate Change and Submerged Resources

Archaeologists are increasingly confronting climate change impacts on terrestrial and coastal cultural sites. There are developing global efforts to understand future impacts and vulnerability, as well as to create management plans to address these impacts. When decisions are made regarding what to do about sites at risk, most approaches involve, as Berenfeld put it, "a 'triage' strategy for cultural heritage management, which requires difficult decisions about what to save and how, as well as recognition that some sites are more important to us than others" (Berenfeld 2015:6). This strategy is playing out around the world, with organizations like Scottish Coastal Archaeology and the Problem of Erosion (SCAPE); and Climate, Heritage and Environments of Reefs, Islands and Headlands (CHERISH) that help document coastal site conditions to assess which sites may be lost, how they may be lost, and whether they can be saved or researched before they are gone.

Effects of climate change on submerged historical resources, in contrast, are poorly understood both in general and by archaeologists themselves although "underwater archaeological sites have the potential to contribute cultural and natural resource data, conservation science, and public outreach initiatives to climate change research" (Wright 2016:256). As Wright notes, "submerged site vulnerabilities ... may be overlooked in the face of terrestrial sites' inundation" (Wright 2016:267). While there is a growing library of information dedicated to managing terrestrial and coastal resources, submerged resources often go undiscussed, which may lead to the incorrect assumption that submerged sites are at less risk because they are already underwater.

With these ideas in mind, FPAN collaborates with partners to track changes to underwater historical resources in Florida. The SHMS Florida program was designed to capture important data about submerged historical resources by teaching citizen divers how to collect quantitative, qualitative, and photographic data using a survey form and specific photography techniques learned during a training course.

Scuba Diving in Florida

Florida has a healthy shipwreck diving economy. There are over 500 shipwrecks documented in state waters that are listed on the Florida Master Site File; more than 60 artificial reefs and potentially 2000 shipwrecks in the Florida Keys alone. Visiting artificial reefs and historical shipwrecks is a popular hobby in the state, and especially in the Florida Keys. Given the abundance of dive sites, year-round diving opportunities, and hundreds of miles of coastline, Florida also has a large number of divers. In 2017 over 13,000 Florida residents earned their Open Water Diver Certification (Diving Equipment and Marketing Association 2018). This is the basic certification that new divers earn, therefore this number does not include any specialty or advanced diving courses, nor does it represent the number of national or international divers who come to Florida to dive.

While there are no definitive numbers of divers who visit shipwrecks in Florida, according to the Florida Bureau of Archaeological Research, of the state's 12 underwater Preserves, there were over 42,000 divers in 2017 (Price 2018). This number does not include the FKNMS Shipwreck Trail or the hundreds of other shipwrecks that are known but are not official preserves in state waters. Economic studies suggest that each year millions of divers enjoy the state's submerged historical resources, adding hundreds of millions of dollars to the state's economy (Diving Equipment and Marketing Association 2013, 2018).

Threats to Florida's Shipwrecks

Human Threats

Florida shipwrecks face many threats, including those from humans. Unintentional harm from divers with poor buoyancy control, an issue most new divers struggle with, can cause divers to accidently come in contact with a shipwreck's structure, and hanging gear can easily rake across the surface of a shipwreck or become entangled. Furthermore, anecdotally, many divers have mentioned being taught by instructors to use shipwreck structure to pull themselves through a shipwreck while earning a shipwreck diver certification. While not all shipwreck diving classes teach these destructive methods, and in fact many are careful to maintain shipwrecks in their condition, there seems to be a wide variety of techniques taught by dive instructors across agencies and around the world.

In addition to unintentional harm, there is the omnipresent but incorrect belief that every shipwreck in Florida contains treasure, a sentiment perpetuated by the few salvage permits that persist in Florida, as well as pop culture 'treasure hunters.' This belief, at its most extreme, is accompanied by destructive methods that are neither careful nor scientific and often include devices like prop wash deflectors to move large amounts of sediment along with any lightweight artifacts that might be buried within, to possibly find heavier precious metals and other heavy objects to be salvaged and often sold.

We now know that shipwrecks and other submerged sites can last hundreds, even thousands of years in the ocean, given the proper circumstances, and that many times shipwrecks reach equilibrium with their surrounding environment. Following the 2001 UNESCO Convention (UNESCO 2017), archaeologists and site managers internationally have moved to a mindset of *in situ* preservation. Lack of proper facilities and funds to conserve, store, or exhibit waterlogged artifacts in perpetuity by most museums and other appropriate facilities, and authenticity of wrecks and artifacts in their submerged context at the site of the historic event all make in situ preservation the primary option for preservation. Submerged historic sites also offer economic benefit to local economies and encourage exploration and conservation.

Systems already in place to protect sites, such as law enforcement, also face challenges. Lack of personnel, difficulty with routinely accessing sites coupled with the "out of sight, out of mind" mentality make submerged historic sites vulnerable. It is often the community of local divers and dive shops that identify and report issues with shipwrecks. While local dive communities may care for and depend on the local shipwrecks for their history and for the economic benefits, it can be difficult to officially report changes to shipwrecks, especially if they are not catastrophic. Many hesitate to go to a federal agency and instead anecdotes are often reported in the newspaper.

Threats of Climate Change

Beyond the direct human impact of treasure hunters, well-intentioned divers, and boaters, which are all threats the state has been dealing with for decades, shipwrecks also face growing threats from climate change. As discussed by Wright (2016), sites that are already submerged are not safe from effects of warming waters, rising seas, ocean acidification, and myriad other precipitous impacts from climate change. Florida's various state and local agencies and governments have a fragmented patchwork of responses to threats of climate change, ranging from denial of its existence, to ambivalence, to creating strong and binding action agreements. Despite the unequal response around the state, effects of climate change are already being documented. While some effects of climate change and changing seas may be beneficial to submerged sites, such as sediment eroded from one area covering another, or sediment burying a site during a storm, both acting to stabilize and protect a shipwreck (Wright 2016:257), monitoring and documentation are essential to defining the effects.

In light of the threats to our submerged historical resources, there is an ongoing effort to educate and engage Floridians and visitors about shipwrecks as a limited and precious resource, and why they should be enjoyed, in situ, for current and future generations, bolstering the dive community and keeping both residents and visitors engaged in the state's submerged history.

Florida's Shipwreck Trails

State and federal agencies have developed shipwreck trails around Florida to engender appreciation for, encourage visitation of, and highlight Florida's unique maritime landscape. Trails include the Florida Underwater Archaeological Preserves, the Panhandle Shipwreck Trail, Biscayne National Park Maritime Heritage Trail, and the FKNMS Shipwreck Trail, together totaling 39 interpreted shipwrecks. These educational tools provide anyone interested with archaeological interpretation of shipwrecks spanning form early Spanish contact, through every major war, and into the modern period. Anyone who is interested in maritime history can appreciate the archaeological information, and divers can use the site maps to better navigate and interpret while diving these shipwrecks.

Shipwreck trails in Florida already help to educate divers and the public about the importance of shipwrecks and their contributions to history. Efforts in education and outreach have also been vital to increasing the value that these sites have to the local community and economy.

The FKNMS, FPAN, and Florida Bureau of Archaeological Research have partnered for years on programming to train the public and dive professionals about responsible diving on shipwrecks and why these nonrenewable resources are important to our state, our country, and the world. These partners and others around the state are constantly striving to make historical resources more accessible to the public, and to engage people directly to instill pride and ownership of these resources.

Submerged HMS Florida Program

In 2016 FPAN developed the HMS Florida program, an integrated community engagement citizen science program, in response to growing threats associated with sea level rise, including erosion, on our coastal sites in Florida. The goal of the program is to "lead to improved management strategies and conservation efforts for archaeological sites" (Miller and Murray 2018:235). Community members are trained to become "scouts" to monitor sites for condition, stability, and indications of threats such as erosion, flooding, or looting.

In 2018, FPAN and FKNMS expanded the HMS Florida program to submerged historic sites, creating the SHMS Florida program. SHMS Florida training seeks to educate the public about basic climate science and submerged historical sites, while engaging them in actively helping to protect sites through monitoring. The program encourages participants to move from passive observation of threats, to engagement in documenting them. SHMS Florida focuses on monitoring sites that are already established shipwreck preserves, which are easily accessible and already interpreted for the general public. Shipwreck trail sites have been fully documented by archaeologists and have been determined to be stable. Scouts can use available educational materials to learn more about the shipwreck before and during their dives and can monitor any of the shipwreck trail sites they choose. FPAN and FKNMS, along with other partners at the Division of Historical Resources inventory office (known as the Florida Master Site File), work diligently to keep sensitive site information confidential, therefore divers are only encouraged to dive publicly known and accessible shipwrecks.

FPAN has a well-established and successful training template for community workshops that includes formal classroom instruction coupled with hands-on field experience. SHMS trainees spend the morning in the classroom with professional staff teaching the basic science of shipwrecks, climate change, and the site's surrounding environment, what risks archaeologists are concerned about and why, and how being a scout can make a difference (Figure 1). The citizen scientists are taught how to collect photographic documentation and what elements of a shipwreck to observe, such as areas of relief where the shipwreck rises above the seabed (Figure 2). Such elements are easily identifiable to any diver on a site and will serve as useful landmarks over time. The entire online monitoring form is reviewed in class so initial questions or comments can be discussed as a group. The goal of the morning session is for attendees to gain: comprehension and familiarity with the site, comfort with the process of collecting data, knowledge of who to contact with questions and legal protection for historical sites, and additional information covering a broad range of topics for them to learn more if they choose.

The afternoon session consists of two dives (weather permitting), during which scouts practice the protocols discussed in the morning session. Before the first dive, instructors distribute sites plans printed on waterproof paper to each diver, and discuss the history and layout

FIGURE 1: FKNMS staff discuss The *City of Washington* shipwreck site during the morning in-class session. (Photo by Brenda Altmeier, February 9, 2019).

FIGURE 2: Scout uses scales to monitor relief section present on The *City of Washington*. (Photo by Rachael Kangas, February 16, 2019).

FIGURE 3: FKNMS staff briefs new SHMS Scouts on the site plan of The *City of Washington* before first dive. (Photo by Rachael Kangas, February 16, 2019).

of the shipwreck site (Figure 3). Instructors prepare divers for what they can expect to see. Both dives are on the same shipwreck, the first dive is for orientation and familiarity with the site, the second for collecting data. Divers are encouraged to take their waterproof site plan to get a general sense of the shipwreck, looking for signs of threats discussed in class, such as rust, storm damage, breakage, etc. The surface interval is spent debriefing, the group discusses together what they saw and where, and any questions are answered by staff. The FPAN staff review the monitoring form to refresh everyone and prepare to document the site during the second dive. During the second dive, citizen scientists are asked to take photos and pay specific attention to factors they are monitoring (Figure 4). After the second dive, FPAN staff work with the new scouts to fill out a master form for the day's monitoring with the group, and discuss any threats noted or questions. Two dives on the same site are preferable to a single dive on two sites for both staff and participants. With scouts still learning, debriefing from the first dive followed by a second visit to the same shipwreck helps clarify the concepts and requirements for the scouts.

While diving the site, scouts note everything including water temperature, potential threats observed, and any changes to the site since their last visit. This data collection will be used to help shape the future of Florida's shipwreck management and will be shared with other sciences to use and compare for their own research questions. The goal is to have written and photographed documentation of sites as they change and are impacted by storms, visitors, and a plethora of other factors. These data can be applied to many different research areas, and will hopefully be integrated into questions about habitat, ocean health, water quality, and any other relevant research.

Outcomes

The first SHMS Florida program was held in June 2018. Since that initial program about 50 submerged scouts have been trained in monitoring procedures resulting in a total of 22 monitoring forms for 18 underwater sites in 10 months. The sites were all characterized in "good" or "fair" condition and low priority; these data are already beneficial for site managers and will be a useful baseline when the next large storm moves through the area.

The future potential for this program and the data collected is enormous. The data collected can be used for multidisciplinary studies from many different fields and will help scientists gain a better understanding of how climate change is affecting submerged cultural sites. For managers, data can be used by Florida's state and federal partners to help track visitation and condition, which will help create management plans and to demonstrate the importance of these sites to the local community. This program can also be used for disaster management and regular upkeep of files. The data collection system is designed to be easy enough to complete that anyone with information about a site feels comfortable using it and in turn will allow land managers to easily update official records. Following major storms, the program can serve as a clearinghouse of information, allowing people to quickly document changes and communicate those changes to archaeologists.

Discussion

Submerged historical resources are threatened by climate change but are often neglected in this discussion. Documentation of the changes to submerged historical resources and their surrounding marine environments is critical in order to aid prioritization and mitigation efforts. Engaging the public in this effort helps foster a sense of stewardship that will contribute to

FIGURE 4: Scout monitors distinct hull section of The *City of Washington*. (Photo by Emily Dietrich, February 16, 2019)

long-term preservation of these sites—divers who visit and document impacts to a site over months or years will be knowledgeable about the site and invested in its protection. Adapting the terrestrial HMS Florida program to submerged historic sites ensures volunteers have skills that can transfer to the terrestrial environment as well, generating a vast potential network of cultural resource 'first responders' able to quickly respond and document sites immediately after storms and flag the most critical sites for archaeologists' response. Working across federal and state lines and fomenting cooperation between preservationists, site managers, dive operators, and other parties is the only way to ensure long-term preservation of the delicate equilibrium necessary to maintain our underwater heritage.

Acknowledgements

The authors wish to thank the staff of FPAN and the FKNMS for their help and support, the University of West Florida, especially FPAN Associate Director, Dr. Della Scott-Ireton whose public outreach efforts in the Keys laid the groundwork for engagement. Thanks to Sarah Miller for conceptualizing HMS Florida. Thanks also to Jeneva Wright for her insight, kindness, and assistance in creating this program. Thanks also to FPAN host institutions, Florida Atlantic University and the University of South Florida. Finally, we wish to thank our scouts, without whom the program would not be possible, especially our top scout, Mako7.

References

BERENFELD, MICHELLE L.
2015   Planning for Permanent Emergency: "Triage" as a Strategy for Managing Cultural Resources Threatened by Climate Change. In *The George Wright Forum*, 32(1): pp. 5-12.

DIVING EQUIPMENT AND MARKETING ASSOCIATION
2013   Fast Facts: Recreational Diving and Snorkeling. Research Reports <https://cdn.ymaws.com/www.dema.org/resource/resmgr/imported/Diving%20Fast%20Facts-2013.pdf>. Accessed 8 March 2019.

DIVING EQUIPMENT AND MARKETING ASSOCIATION
2018   Fast Facts: Recreational Diving and Snorkeling. Research Reports <https://www.dema.org/store/download.aspx?id=7811B097-8882-4707-A160-F999B49614B6>. Accessed 8 March 2019.

MILLER, SARAH, AND EMILY JANE MURRAY
2018   Heritage Monitoring Scouts: Engaging the Public to Monitor Sites at Risk Across Florida. *Conservation and Management of Archaeological Sites* 20(4):234-260.

PRICE, MELISSA
2018   Florida's Underwater Archaeological Preserves 2017 Conditions Report. Florida Division of Historical Resources.

UNESCO
2017   Underwater Cultural Heritage: About the Convention of the Protection of the Underwater Cultural Heritage. United Nations Educational, Scientific, and Cultural Organization <http://www.unesco.org/new/en/culture/themes/underwater-cultural-heritage/2001-convention/>. Accessed 9 April 2019.

WRIGHT, JENEVA
2016   Maritime Archaeology and Climate Change: An Invitation. *Journal of Maritime Archaeology* 11:255-270.

················

Rachael Kangas
2211 Widman Way, Suite 230
Fort Myers, Florida 33901
(239) 223-6865
rkangas@fau.edu

Jeffrey Moates
4202 E. Fowler Ave, SOC 110
Tampa, FL 33620
(941) 704-2521
jmoates@usf.edu

Brenda Altmeier
P.O. Box 1083
Key Largo, FL 33037
(305) 434-9386
brenda.altmeier@noaa.gov

Sara Ayers-Rigsby
111 East Las Olas Blvd
Ft. Lauderdale, FL 33301
(954) 254-9657
sayersrigsby@fau.edu

30 Years Later: Revisiting the 1733 *San Pedro* and *San Felipe* Shipwrecks in the Florida Keys

Samuel I. Haskell, Tori L. Galloway, Matthew Lawrence, Charles D. Beeker, Kirsten M. Hawley

In 1988, Indiana University (IU) assisted the State of Florida in the survey of the 1733 San Pedro *and* San Felipe *shipwrecks with the goal of selecting a candidate for the creation of an underwater preserve. In April 1989, the San Pedro Underwater Archaeological Preserve State Park was opened to the public. Since that time, IU has conducted periodic assessments of the preserve in order to provide archaeological and biological monitoring information to resource managers. These shipwrecks continue to support diverse assemblages of marine organisms that are representative of one of Florida's oldest artificial reefs. This paper presents observations and data collected after 30 years of monitoring efforts, as well as recommendations for future management of the* San Pedro *and* San Felipe *shipwrecks.*

Historical Background

Following the Spanish colonization of the New World in the early 16th century, tremendous amounts of exotic New World commodities were transported across the Atlantic, back to Spain. In order to protect the Spanish convoy system from European rivals, armed escort galleons would accompany the convoy, ensuring safe passage of all goods and ships on their return to Spain. Following the collection of New World goods from South and Central America, the Spanish ships would typically rendezvous in Havana, Cuba. After departing Havana, these ships would sail through the Straits of Florida, where they were then pushed northward by the Gulf Stream, navigating between the treacherous reefs of the Bahamas and Florida Keys (Beeker 2003). Once the ships' navigators determined they had skirted the shoal waters, the fleet would alter course to Bermuda and catch the westerly trade winds across the Atlantic (Beeker 1994; Smith 1988).

San Pedro and *San Felipe* departed Havana with a fleet of other vessels led by Lieutenant-General Rodrigo de Torres on Friday, July 13th, 1733. Within the fleet's holds were 12.4 million pesos in silver, gold, and general cargo from the New World. In sight of the Florida Keys after only a day of sailing, shifting winds alerted the fleet to an approaching storm. By the following day, the vessels were caught in a hurricane that resulted in the loss of *San Pedro* and *San Felipe*, along with most of the fleet (Beeker and James 1996; Contratación 2901 1733).

Spanish archival records state that a salvage squadron was quickly dispatched from Havana to aid the fleet. By August 3rd, 1733, much of the cargo had been salvaged and prepared for transport back to Cuba. Several of the vessels were refloated, but at least 15 vessels were burned to the waterline to facilitate the salvage of the ships' cargos (Contratación 2977 1734; Contratación 5102 1733). The salvors were able to recover the registered gold and silver, as well as a substantial amount of goods that were unregistered on the original manifests (Beeker 2003: 8-9; Contratación 2003 1734; Contratación 5147 1733; Marx 1987; Meylach 1971; Skowronek 1982; Smith and Dunbar 1997).

Treasure Hunting Impacts

In addition to the original Spanish salvage immediately following the loss of the fleet intended to recover lost goods that could still be used, the shipwreck sites of the 1733 fleet were heavily impacted by modern treasure hunting efforts, ultimately ravaging the site for artillery and treasure. In the early 1960s, treasure hunting in Florida boomed with the discovery of the 1715 plate fleet off Vero Beach (Throckmorton 1990). People flocked to the Florida Keys to pursue the 1733 fleet's perceived riches but unlike the 1715 fleet, less gold and silver has been discovered on the remains of these ships due to the success of the original Spanish salvage efforts.

Archaeological Investigations and Preserve Establishment

Members of Florida's Underwater Research Section, now the Bureau of Archaeological Research, conducted the first substantial archaeological investigation of the 1733 shipwrecks in 1977. The goal of this original survey was to "examine the sites of eight merchant ships in state waters and to establish the nature and extent of existing wreckage" (Smith et al. 1990). The eight shipwreck sites surveyed in the 1977 field season include

Capitana, Infante, Herrera, San Pedro, Tres Puentes, San Jose, Chaves, and *Nuestra Señora de las Angustias.*

Eleven years later, in 1988, under the direction of Florida's State Underwater Archaeologist Roger Smith, IU assisted in the survey and inspection of several of the 1733 shipwrecks with the goal of selecting a candidate for the creation of a new Florida marine protected area. This designation would establish the site as both an archaeological preserve and public shipwreck park. Each shipwreck received a score based on the following criteria: visibility, currents, aquatic life, coral structure, ballast, intrusive features, location, research potential, and overall park potential. The collaborative team of researchers narrowed their search down to two likely candidates: *San Pedro* and *San Felipe* (Beeker 2003; Maus et al. 2015).

FIGURE 1: Cement replica cannons on the 1733 San Pedro Underwater Archaeological Preserve (Indiana University, 2018).

Approximately one mile offshore from Lower Matecumbe Key, *San Felipe* rests in just 6 meters of water. Oriented northwest by southeast, *San Felipe* is characterized by a large, relatively intact ballast pile in a white sand patch surrounded by seagrass. The 2 meter high and relatively intact portion of the ballast pile on the *San Felipe* can be attributed to the fact that the modern treasure salvors had little success working on the site and eventually abandoned it for other shipwrecks (Meylach 1971).

San Pedro received much more attention from treasure hunters than *San Felipe*. These treasure hunters fragmented its ballast mound and recovered cannons, as well as remnants of cargo, elements of the ship's rigging and hardware, and thousands of coins dated between 1731 and 1733 (NOAA 2017; Smith 1988). Fortunately, *San Pedro*'s wooden hull was not fully disarticulated in the process and remains preserved in sediment. The site's location, farther away from shore, resulted in generally good visibility and an abundance of corals, invertebrates, and fish that now inhabit the site, creating interest for visiting divers.

Ultimately, archaeologists selected *San Pedro* as the best candidate for an underwater park as it had "outstanding" potential for public visitation (Smith et al. 1990). While *San Pedro*'s precious metals had been stripped away, most of the lower hull was still intact. To protect this hull and prepare the site for park development, researchers reconsolidated the ballast stones into a single pile to serve as the central component of the preserve.

In addition to rebuilding the ballast pile, *San Pedro* Underwater Archaeological Preserve was enhanced with the addition of seven replica concrete cannons (Figure 1) and an iron anchor recovered by treasure hunters from one of the 1733 fleet shipwrecks. A limestone monument with a bronze plaque relating *San Pedro*'s story and its preserve designation, was placed on the site to enhance visitors' experience and generate increased awareness of *San Pedro*'s historical and ecological significance. Six mooring buoys were installed in a ring around the shipwreck, as well as a spar marker buoy- responsible for alerting boaters to the preserve. In April 1989, the *San Pedro* Underwater Archaeological Preserve officially opened to the public. *San Pedro*'s rich history and biodiversity, as well as its close proximity to the state parks on Lignumvitae Key and Indian Key, made the park a popular attraction for snorkelers, diving charters and sportfishing guides (Beeker 1988a; Beeker 1988b; Florida Department of State 2005).

While *San Felipe* was not chosen for preserve status at the time, it was listed on the National Register for Historic Places in 1994, following several more seasons of fieldwork by IU. Given the success of the *San Pedro* Underwater Archaeological Preserve, designating *San Felipe* as such may realize greater protection and enjoyment of the shipwreck. As the best remaining example of the 1733 fleet, *San Felipe* could be a valuable tool for building resource stewardship and educating divers about its importance to Florida history.

Shipwrecks as Underwater Preserves – Thirty Years of Long-Term Monitoring Data

As a State Park, *San Pedro* Underwater Archaeological Preserve is a successful marine protected area. Its mooring buoys and shallow depth allow snorkeling visitors to enjoy the site, where they experience a piece of history and view diverse marine life. Although *San Pedro* does not appear to be sustaining long-term, large coral growth, the abundant invertebrates and fish are evidence of its successful role as an inshore patch reef. *San Pedro* is a prime example of a marine protected area, conserving both underwater cultural heritage and associated marine organisms while promoting sustainable tourism. Since the initial 1988 IU survey of the 1733 shipwreck sites, IU has returned to *San Felipe* and *San Pedro* on 10 other occasions to document the shipwrecks' archaeological and biological resources. This long history of site monitoring gives archaeologists and resource managers a large collection of long-term, archival data from numerous past research projects over the last 30 years.

San Pedro and *San Felipe* support a diverse assemblage of marine organisms characteristic of an inshore patch reef community. During IU and NOAA's 2018 collaborative assessment, numerous schooling fish and invertebrates were observed on the sites. Since the ballast pile was loosely reconsolidated on *San Pedro*, the disarticulated stone substrate is not conducive to long-term coral stability and growth. The low-lying ballast stone pile provides substrate for numerous coral and sponge recruits, however long-term growth appears to be regularly disrupted by sedimentation and movement caused from hurricanes and other wave-causing events (Hawley et al. 2018).

Comparison of archival site documentation records with the results of frequent archaeological investigations reveals how *San Pedro* and *San Felipe* have changed over the last 30 years. By looking at specific coral clusters as designated biological monitoring stations (Figure 2), biologists can assess the long-term health of a shipwreck's associated biological resources by returning to these locations in subsequent years. From an archaeological perspective, these data also allow for comprehensive assessment of changes and impacts to these sites through time. This information provides a better understanding of recent site formation processes and can aid resource managers in determining how to mitigate future effects.

Photogrammetric Monitoring

Over the past thirty years, IU researchers have been documenting site changes on both the 1733 *San Felipe* shipwreck site and the 1733 *San Pedro* Underwater Archaeological Preserve. When researchers began the baseline monitoring of these sites, data was stored in the form of 35mm slides and hand-drawn site maps. Now, evolving technology allows us to record entire sites in a single dive, using relatively inexpensive cameras and a small crew. This technology, known as computer-vision photogrammetry, uses two-dimensional images to build three-dimensional models. Photogrammetric models can be analyzed for change and easily shared between institutions using websites like Sketchfab. Because of the immersive nature of the model, it is also especially good at showcasing submerged cultural heritage to those that might not otherwise have access. When used alongside archival data from the past thirty years, these evolving

FIGURE 2: Photograph of a coral cluster on the San Felipe taken in 1992 (left) and the same coral cluster viewed in a 3D photogrammetric model of the site created in 2018 (right) (Indiana University).

new technologies are invaluable to monitoring and management of underwater cultural heritage.

In July 2015, IU returned to the 1733 *San Pedro* shipwreck to create highly accurate 3D models and photomosaics to serve as new monitoring baselines for future management. Additionally, this project served as a general demonstration for the Florida Keys National Marine Sanctuary (FKNMS) on the use of photogrammetric methodology as part of an improved rapid-assessment protocol for submerged cultural and biological resources (Maus et al. 2015). The central data collection technique for this project was structure-from-motion photogrammetric imagery acquisition, accomplished by divers using open circuit SCUBA and GoPro cameras to collect images while swimming designated transects across the site (Maus et al. 2015, 2017; Van Damme 2015a, 2015b). Prior to starting photo transects, divers deployed photobars to establish scale and estimate average error in the finished model (Maus et al. 2015).

Images were edited in Adobe Lightroom for color correction and dehazing, prior to processing in Agisoft Photoscan. Photoscan automatically detects and corrects GoPro lens distortion, and its algorithm filters out most mobile subjects such as fish and other marine life. Images are processed in chunks using standard workflow commands to generate a sparse point cloud, dense point cloud, textured model, and tiled model (Agisoft 2016). The final site model from the 2015 *San Pedro* fieldwork was composed of 1,770 images and had an estimated error of 1.3935 cm (Maus et al. 2015). Additional images of key site features, such as Cannon #7 and Coral Cluster #5, were collected by divers for future processing. Since image acquisition is typically the limiting factor in photogrammetric modeling, divers were able to collect supplemental photos for future research and archival cataloging.

The photogrammetric methodology employed in this assessment was designed to be inexpensive and quick, while simultaneously providing high quality, detailed imagery and volumetric data. The fieldwork component of this process was efficient enough to permit imagery collection from multiple sites in a single day. As such, it would be feasible and beneficial to employ this

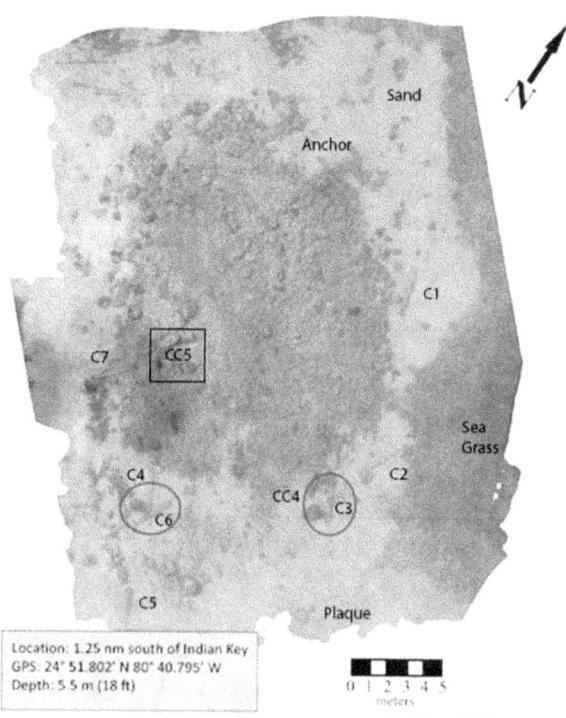

FIGURE 3: Photogrammetric site plans of the San Pedro from 2015 and 2018. Note significant movement of cannons (circled) and large amounts of newly exposed ballast (Indiana University, 2018).

photogrammetric monitoring technique regularly as part of a rapid assessment protocol to closely track changes in submerged cultural and biological resources with a very high degree of accuracy and detailed resolution (Hawley et al. 2018).

Hurricane Irma

Following Hurricane Irma's landfall in the lower Florida Keys in September 2017, IU and NOAA researchers returned to *San Pedro* and *San Felipe* to record observations and assess the condition of the sites. Additionally, the same structure-from-motion computer-vision photogrammetry used during the 2015 assessment was used in 2018 to produce updated orthomosaic site plans and three-dimensional models. These models were used to analyze changes in the sites from the 2015 assessment, and provide a baseline monitoring reference for future work.

The impacts of Hurricane Irma are clearly seen on both *San Pedro* and *San Felipe* (Figure 3). Several of the replica cement cannons placed around *San Pedro* moved between 2015 and 2018. Due to the lesser density of cement as compared to iron, these replica cannons weigh far less than iron guns. Comparison of 2015 and 2018 photogrammetric site plans revealed significant movement (>3 meters) of cannon #3 and cannon #6. Cannon #4 was relocated onto the ballast stones between cannon #6 and cannon #7, which were all shifted during the 2018 hurricane. Only cannon #2 and cannon #7 showed no movement. Sand movement on *San Pedro* also exposed disarticulated ballast stones and previously buried buoy anchor blocks. Cannon #5, documented as buried by IU from 2003 to 2015, was also uncovered.

FIGURE 4: IU's Charles Beeker (right) and Tori Galloway (left) examine newly exposed wood on *San Felipe* following Hurricane Irma (Matthew Lawrence, 2018).

Hurricane impacts on *San Felipe* are most obviously visible on the southeast side of the site, where a significant number of wood pieces were uncovered and are now disarticulated on the surface (Figure 4). This wood should be reburied as soon as possible to avoid any degradation of the archaeological resources. Since there were no photogrammetric models created of *San Felipe* prior to the 2018 field season, it is not possible to asses minute changes in ballast structure with the same detail as on *San Pedro*. While comparison with archival photographs indicates some movement of ballast stones around the site, this highlights the need for the usage of highly accurate photogrammetric models in long-term site monitoring to provide more quantitative data.

Despite these disturbances, overall the two sites appear stable (Galloway et al. 2019; Hawley et al. 2018). The photogrammetric results from these projects should be considered for use as a continued baseline for monitoring the *San Pedro* Underwater Archaeological Preserve and *San Felipe*. As an added benefit, the accessible and detailed photogrammetric models produced by this process have excellent potential as tools for public outreach and education, and for comparing other site changes pre and post-hurricane.

Conclusions

Over thirty years of monitoring *San Pedro* and *San Felipe* allows for a long-term assessment of the complex changes over time affecting submerged cultural and biological resources in the Florida Keys. New, readily implemented, photogrammetric methodologies offer even better information with which to examine environmental and anthropogenic impacts. Long-term monitoring, like that undertaken by IU, provides resource managers with the best information to ensure the protection and preservation of underwater cultural heritage and the marine organisms that give it new life and broad interest.

Acknowledgements

This project was made possible through the support of Quiescence Diving Services and owner Rob Bleser, Zach Wagner, Dr. Claudia Johnson, Dr. Bill Ruf, the 2018 IU FKNMS Field School, and the numerous IU students participating in this research over the years. Additionally, the authors would like to thank the Florida Division of Historical Resources and NOAA's FKNMS Maritime Heritage Program for their support over the last 30 years of ongoing research.

References

Agisoft LLC
2016 Agisoft Photoscan User Manual: Professional Edition, Version 1.2. St. Petersburg, Russia.

Beeker, Charles D.
1988a New Florida Underwater Shipwreck Park. *The Undersea Journal* 2:29.

1988b Shipwrecks: A Changing Perspective. *The Undersea Journal* 2:44-43.

1994 *San Felipe* Historic Shipwreck Nomination National Register for Historic Places. Manuscript on file, Florida National Registration Review Board, Tallahassee, Florida.

2003 *San Felipe* 1733 Spanish Shipwreck: A Call to Preserve a Unique Submerged Cultural and Biological Resource. M.A. Thesis, Department of Anthropology, Indiana University, Bloomington, Indiana.

Beeker, Charles D., and S.R. James
1996 *San Felipe* Report. Report to Florida Department of State, Division of Historical Resources, Bureau of Archaeological Research, Tallahassee, Florida.

Contratación 2901
1733 Libro 2. Folios 198, 204v-205v. Libro de Registro. Monroe County Public Library, Islamorada, Florida.

Contratación 5102
1733 [Microfilm Reel #4]. Monroe County Public Library, Islamorada, Florida.

Contratación 5147
1733 [Microfilm Reel #2]. Monroe County Public Library, Islamorada, Florida.

Contratación 2003
1734 [Microfilm, Reel #2, 11]. Monroe County Public Library, Islamorada, Florida.

Contratación 2977
1734 Document 6. Monroe County Public Library, Islamorada, Florida.

Contratación 5072
1734 [Microfilm Reel #2, 8]. Monroe County Public Library, Islamorada, Florida. Deagan, K. A.

Florida Department of State
2005 1733 Spanish Galleon Trail. Florida Department of State Division of Historical Resources. < http://info.flheritage.com/galleon-trail/> Accessed 13 April 2019.

Galloway, Tori L., Matthew Lawrence, Charles D. Beeker, Samuel I. Haskell, Kirsten Hawley
2019 Documenting Historic Shipwrecks in the 21st Century: Using New and Old Data to Support Monitoring of the 1733 San Pedro and San Felipe. Poster presented at the 2019 Society for Historical Archaeology Conference in St. Charles, Missouri.

Hawley, Kirsten M., C. Beeker, T. Galloway, S. Haskell, C. Johnson, A. Lagunas
2018 Photogrammetric Assessment of the 1733 *San Pedro* Underwater Archaeological Preserve and the 1733 *San Felipe* Shipwreck Sites following Hurricane Irma. Submitted to: Florida Division of Historical Resources, Florida Division of Recreation and Parks, and NOAA Florida Keys National Marine Sanctuary.

Marx, Robert
1987 Shipwrecks in the Americas. Dover, Toronto.

Meylach, Martin
1971 Diving to a Flash of Gold. Florida Classics Library, Port Salemo, Florida.

Maus, Matthew, Charles Beeker, Mylana Haydu, and Samuel I. Haskell
2015 Application of Photogrammetry for Assessment and Monitoring of the 1733 *San Pedro* Underwater Archaeological Preserve. Report to Florida Division of Historical Resources (Bureau of Archaeological Research), Florida Division of Recreation and Parks (Bureau of Natural and Cultural Resources), and NOAA Florida Keys National Marine Sanctuary from Indiana University Center for Underwater Science, Bloomington, IN.

Maus, Matthew, Denise Jaffke, Samuel I. Haskell
2017 Photogrammetry as a Tool for Monitoring Submerged Cultural Resources: The Emerald Bay State Park Workshop. In *Society for California Archaeology Proceedings*, Volume 31, Reddy, Seetha, Allika Ruby, Heather Baron, Sherri Andrews, Shelly Davis-King, Sharon Waechter editors, pp. 58-79. Society for California Archaeology, Chico, CA.

NOAA
2017 The *San Pedro*. NOAA Florida Keys National Marine Sanctuary. <https://floridakeys.noaa.gov/shipwrecktrail/sanpedro.html> Accessed 11 April 2019

Skowronek, Russel K.
1982 Trade Patterns of 18th Century Frontier New Spain: The 1733 Flota and St. Augustine. M.A. thesis, Department of Anthropology, Florida State University, Tallahassee, FL.

SMITH, ROGER C.
1988   A Proposal to Establish an Underwater Archaeological Preserve in the Florida Keys. Manuscript on file, Florida Department of State, Division of Historical Resources, Bureau of Archaeological Research, Tallahassee, Florida.

SMITH, ROGER C. AND J. DUNBAR
1977   An Underwater Archaeological Survey of Eight Spanish Merchant Naos of the 1733 New Spain Fleet. Manuscript on file, Florida Department of State, Division of Historical Resources, Bureau of Archaeological Research, Tallahassee, Florida.

SMITH, ROGER C., ROBERT FINEGOLD, AND ERIC STEPHENS
1990   Establishing an Underwater Archaeological Preserve in the Florida Keys: A Case Study. APT Bulletin Vol 22 No 3, p11-18. Association for Preservation Technology International, Springfield, Illinois.

THROCKMORTON, PETER
1990   The World's Worst Investment: The Economics of Treasure Hunting with Real-Life Comparisons. In *Underwater Archaeology Proceedings from the Society for Historical Archaeology Conference* 1990, Carrell, Toni L., editor, pp. 6-10. Society for Historical Archaeology, Tucson, Arizona.

VAN DAMME, THOMAS
2015a Computer Vision Photogrammetry for Underwater Archaeological Site Recording: A Critical Assessment. Master's thesis, Maritime Archaeology Programme, University of Southern Denmark, Odense, Denmark.

2015b Computer Vision Photogrammetry for Underwater Archaeological Site Recording in Low-Visibility Environment. *The International Archives of the Photogrammetry, Remote Sensing and Spatial Information Sciences* XL-5/W5, pp. 231-238. Piano di Sorrento, Italy.

· · · · · · · · · · · · · · · ·

Samuel I. Haskell
1025 E 7th St, Room 112J
Bloomington, Indiana 47405
sihaskel@indiana.edu
Work: (812) 856-2360
Cell: (812) 322-9976

Tori L. Galloway
1025 E 7th St, Room 058
Bloomington, Indiana 47405
torgallo@indiana.edu
Work: (812) 856-2360

Matthew Lawrence
95230 Oversees Hwy
Key Largo, Florida 33037
Matthew.lawrence@noaa.gov
Work: (305)434-9383

Charles D. Beeker
1025 E 7th St, Room 058
Bloomington, Indiana 47405
cbeeker@indiana.edu
Work: (812) 856-5748

Kirsten M. Hawley
1025 E 7th St, Room 058
Bloomington, Indiana 47405
kmhawley@indiana.edu
Work: (812) 856-2360

In Situ Digital Documentation of the 1559 Emanuel Point Shipwrecks

Micah B. Minnocci, Hunter W. Whitehead

Since 1996, University of West Florida (UWF) archaeologists have documented the vessels associated with Tristán de Luna y Arellano's 1559 colonization fleet. In recent years, UWF documentation methods evolved to include photographs and video of excavation units. This allows archaeologists to compare digital images with diver-created illustrations. Further technological advances, such as computer-vision photogrammetric software, permit archaeologists to preserve minute details of archaeological sites. The development of digital documentation methods utilized by UWF archaeologists on the Emanuel Point Shipwrecks are discussed here.

Introduction

In 1989, the University of West Florida (UWF) held its first maritime archaeological field school, which focused on documentation of the Deadman's Island shipwreck (8SR782) (Smith 2018b:9). The 1990 and 1992 pilot surveys for shipwrecks in Pensacola Bay conducted by the Florida Bureau of Archaeological Research (BAR) were the catalysts for the development of UWF's program in maritime archaeology (Smith et al. 1995:xii). During these surveys, BAR discovered over 45 historic shipwrecks dating from Spanish, British, and American occupations of Pensacola (Smith 2018b:3). Perhaps the most significant of these discoveries is a vessel associated with Tristán de Luna y Arellano's 1559 colonization fleet, referred to as Emanuel Point I (8ES1980). Since the discovery of Emanuel Point I, UWF archaeologists and field school students have been regularly involved with the study of Pensacola's underwater cultural heritage.

The 1992 discovery of the Emanuel Point I shipwreck cemented UWF's involvement in maritime archaeology. In 1993, students from UWF participated in a BAR-sponsored field school focused on the excavation and interpretation of the Emanuel Point I shipwreck. Since 1997, UWF instructors have held a maritime field school every summer to date (Bratten 2012:10). Florida Division of Historical Resources special category grants allowed UWF's discovery of two additional Luna shipwrecks: Emanuel Point II (8ES3345) in 2006, and Emanuel Point III (8ES4360) in 2016.

Roughly three decades of UWF maritime archaeology have witnessed hundreds of field school students, but also significant changes in technology and methods. For example, UWF's underwater photography capabilities advanced from 35mm cameras to digital cameras in 2001 and added *GoPro Hero* cameras in 2011. This technological advancement certainly increased the number of photographs taken on underwater sites with the elimination of the cost and time involved in developing film. Furthermore, the accessibility of a cost-efficient 3D photogrammetric software package, Agisoft's *Photoscan*, allowed for supplementary documentation and analysis techniques. Changes to UWF's digital recording techniques over time are discussed here, as well as the usefulness of 3D photogrammetry methods as a comparative tool.

Brief Historical Background of the 1559 Luna Settlement

On June 11, 1559, Tristán de Luna y Arellano's 12-ship fleet, carrying 1,500 colonists, departed Veracruz, Mexico for what is now known as Pensacola, Florida. The fleet arrived in Pensacola Bay on August 14, 1559 with abundant supplies to establish a Spanish colony. King Phillip II intended to build one colony in Pensacola, a second colony inland at the native province of Coosa, and a third on the coast of current-day South Carolina (Worth 2018:34). These three colonies would inhibit French colonization attempts in the region while also providing, to some extent, an overland highway from the Atlantic to the Gulf of Mexico.

Upon arrival, the colonists offloaded the supplies and equipment necessary to build a settlement, although the food stores remained on the moored vessels (Worth 2018:47). The decision to leave food aboard resulted in disaster for the colonization attempt. During initial development and exploration of the local environment a hurricane swept through Pensacola and devastated nearly the entire fleet. Six ships were driven aground and sunk, leaving the fledgling settlement with considerably less supplies. Luna immediately sent a ship back to Mexico to convey the settlement's situation and request for aid.

The settlement faced numerous hardships over the next two years until its demise. Despite provisions supplied to the colonists from Mexico and Havana, many colonists died of starvation and sickness. Attempts to trade with local natives were rarely successful and desperate Spanish colonists eventually questioned Luna's leadership (Worth 2018:56). Upon receiving several formal complaints, the Viceroy of New Spain ordered Luna to return to Spain. Shortly after, the remaining Spanish colonists abandoned the failed settlement. University of West Florida archaeologist John Worth notes that the settlement survived for a little over two years, marking the longest European occupation of the continental United States to date (Worth 2018:59). A more detailed account of Luna's colonization attempt may be found in Roger Smith's (2018a) edited volume *Florida's Lost Galleon: The Emanuel Point Shipwreck*.

The Development of Photogrammetry in Underwater Archaeology

In recent years, the use of 3D photogrammetric modeling methods in underwater archaeology has risen dramatically. During the 2016 Society for Historical and Underwater Archaeology conference there were three presentations which included photogrammetry of underwater cultural material (Society for Historical Archaeology 2016). At the 2017 conference, the number of photogrammetry presentations increased to fifteen (Society for Historical Archaeology 2017). This rise in utilization is in part due to the availability of cost-effective photogrammetric software packages. However, photogrammetry is certainly not new to the field of underwater archaeology.

Underwater archaeologists have utilized photogrammetry as early as George Bass' experiments in the 1960s (Drap 2012). The ability to create 3D imagery from 3D photographs was undoubtedly appealing to those formulating the best methods for shipwreck documentation. Technological advances such as computers and software capable of triangulating tri-dimensional data further improved photogrammetric methods. In the early 21st century, newly developed multi-image photogrammetry software prompted archaeologists to begin testing new site documentation procedures (Drap 2012; McCarthy and Benjamin 2014). Within the last ten years, the multi-image photogrammetry software *Photoscan* has been utilized by numerous archaeologists on underwater sites (for example, see Burgess 2013; Balletti et al. 2015; Aragon et al. 2018).

Kotaro Yamafune developed photogrammetric methods for underwater archaeological sites using *Photoscan* for his PhD dissertation at Texas A&M University (Yamafune 2016). His dissertation study involved testing data acquisition, data processing, and data analysis methods. In 2014 Yamafune visited the University of West Florida to teach these approaches to graduate students in the Division of Anthropology and Archaeology. With his guidance, UWF master's candidate Hunter Whitehead adapted these methods to the ongoing excavation of the Emanuel Point II shipwreck. In a recent conversation, Kotaro Yamafune (2019, pers. comm.) explained the rapid advances in photogrammetric software. *Photoscan* is now, as of 2018, called Metashape and requires a new set of protocols. Furthermore, he explained that there are new software packages that have outpaced Metashape's capabilities. These advances illustrate how quickly technology can alter the documentation and interpretation methods of archaeological sites.

Photogrammetric Methods

Yamafune's (2016) methods heavily influenced those described here, although some techniques were altered to meet site-specific conditions. Multi-image photogrammetry is essentially the process of creating 3D spatial data from a series of overlapping photographs. *Photoscan* determines similarities of the pixel data in this series of photographs and renders a 3D point cloud similar to data created by laser scanning technology. The photogrammetric process utilized during the 2015-2016 Emanuel Point II and III excavations included three broad steps: 1) photograph data acquisition, 2) photogrammetric post-processing, and 3) analysis of resulting data.

Emanuel Point II lies in Pensacola Bay in about 12 feet of water under fine silty sediment mixed with clay textures. During the winter months, there were days of virtually surface-to-sea floor visibility. On the other hand, after heavy rains, visibility sometimes dropped to nearly zero. The range in visibility required divers to utilize *GoPro Hero* cameras to capture video instead of single photographs. The Cultural Heritage Agency of the Netherlands utilized this technique during the excavation of the Straatvaarder wreck, where visibility was as low as 50 centimeters (Van Damme 2015:233). Video captured very close to the wreck in a low-visibility environment allowed for the acquisition of the necessary series of high quality, overlapping images.

Test excavations on Emanuel Point III have benefitted from a somewhat clearer water environment. The wreck lies in about 8 feet of water in a sandy sediment. Even though Emanuel Point III lies only half of a mile away from Emanuel Point II, the visibility was close to 8 feet on most days, likely due to the difference in sediment type. For consistency, divers took a similar video acquisition approach during excavations. Video height for both Emanuel Point II and III was restricted because of an overlying aluminum bar grid system consisting of 1 x 1 meter units. This grid system was part of the excavation plan, though was an undesirable obstruction for video or photogrammetric models.

University of West Florida archaeologists and students utilized underwater videography on Emanuel Point II prior to their intent to utilize photogrammetric methods. However, a standard operating procedure for the video of excavation units had not yet been formed. The video collected at that time consisted of both fully and partially excavated units, and generally was taken from a bird's-eye view. A high-quality 3D model normally requires images from various angles of the object; however, the authors were able to post-process several videos from previous field seasons. The successful modeling adapted from older videos likely stemmed from the low profile of the shipwreck. During the 2015 and 2016 field seasons, divers collected video from at least two sides of each unit to enhance *Photoscan*'s capability to produce a 3D model.

The post-processing of video data for the creation of photogrammetric data consisted of several broad steps. First, the conversion of video data to still images was necessary to create a series of overlapping photographs. The resulting images were then visually enhanced in Adobe *Photoshop*, and then uploaded into Photoscan for photogrammetric processing. These steps are described in Yamafune's (2016) dissertation; however, some steps were altered to fit data quality limitations.

In most cases, the video-to-stills conversion process produces a lower quality resolution than individual photographs. As mentioned previously, however, the low-visibility environment around Emanuel Point II necessitates the use of video. Macroplant's open source software, *Adapter*, allowed the extraction of still images from video at a designated frame rate. To reduce the number of blurry images due to quick video movement of divers, the frame rate was set at three images per second. Any resulting blurry images were then deleted from the sequence prior to the image correction process in *Photoshop*. There are numerous image correction techniques within *Photoshop*. The authors chose a minimalist approach of utilizing the dehazing and sharpening features. These tools dramatically increased the contrast of the images and allowed for cross-referenced pixel recognition in *Photoscan*. While the images can be further refined in *Photoshop*, this minimalist approach resulted in quicker processing times. Additionally, as there were usually 300-400 images per video, *Photoshop*'s batch-processing feature saved the authors countless hours.

Upon achieving the desired image quality, the series of images was uploaded into *Photoscan*. The software's essential steps consist of aligning the sequence of images, building a point cloud, overlaying a mesh, and finalizing the texture. These steps can sometimes take numerous hours of processing time and often a recognizable model does not come into fruition. Each of the main software processing steps allow for low, medium, and high settings. To best utilize time, the authors first processed each model on the lowest settings to ensure the model was feasible. If a point cloud resembling the site is created on lower settings, higher settings are utilized to further refine the model. The authors also tested the unaltered images through this process, which generally led to lower quality results. Finally, an orthophoto, which is essentially a photomosaic of the 3D model, was generated within *Photoscan*. These images were manipulated in *Photoshop* to create sketch-like illustrations for comparison to diver-created sketches and photographs.

Results and Discussion

The author utilized data from the 2014 through 2016 field seasons to test photogrammetric modeling techniques, which included a total of 120 videos of excavation units. Only 34 of these videos underwent photogrammetric processing, while 32 were modeled successfully. To establish which videos had 3D-modeling potential, a Microsoft Office *Excel* spreadsheet was developed to serve as a working document for future archaeologists. The spreadsheet notes the UWF video file name, the excavation unit number, video color/hue, and any additional comments. The video color is included since the visibility and hue of the water on Emanuel Point II changed dramatically between green, yellow, and brown during the three field seasons. The hue and color of the water severely influenced the model quality, and green hues were generally easier to model than brown hues.

The 2015-2016 UWF field seasons focused on the midship and stern sections of Emanuel Point II. Key features of these sections include the main mast step, the stern post, and disarticulated upper ship structure located aft of the main hull assembly. Several UWF theses, completed and ongoing, concentrated on these features.

One of these theses, completed by Charles Bendig, focused on the main mast step and virtual reconstruction of the pump well components utilizing photogrammetric methods (Bendig 2016). Another student, Stephen Atkinson, undertook the analysis of the aft section of the ship and created a photogrammetric model of the stern post (Atkinson 2017). Andrew Willard is currently working on documenting the disarticulated upper structure components aft of the main hull assembly (Willard, forthcoming). The authors of this paper generated and analyzed 3D photogrammetric models of both the midship and stern sections of Emanuel Point II and compared them to the diver-generated sketches and plan view drawings.

Most of the 3D models generated depict shipwreck structure within 1 x 1 meter units; however, some models provide an overview of multiple units. One example is a 3 x 3 meter unit, which was opened to investigate the main mast step. Attempts were made to video this area for the creation of a 3D model; however, the unit was usually too silted out to collect adequate footage. One partially successful 3D model was generated but had numerous obvious discrepancies. Comparisons to Bendig's (2016) plan drawing of the main mast step demonstrated that diver created measurements and sketches were the better documentation method in this case. Atkinson's (2017) 3D model of the sternpost exhibited less accuracy than his plan drawing, however visibility in this feature of the shipwreck was significantly less due to the depth of the unit. Other units, such as those studied by Willard (forthcoming), are under much less sediment allowing for better video collection, and thus better 3D models.

Most 3D models generated during this study portrayed accurate representations similar to diver-generated unit drawings of the shipwreck structure. However, some 3D models displayed more wood degradation than the unit drawings. Video collection in past field seasons was a lower priority and was completed much later than diver-created drawings. As a result, inconsistencies were observed between 3D models and unit drawings demonstrating how quickly the shipwreck degrades during excavation. Findings of this study demonstrate that photogrammetric models may capture minute details that are otherwise missed by divers in low-visibility conditions.

Several research obstacles arose during photogrammetric testing; some of these were anticipated, such as low visibility and poor video quality, others were less expected. The use of white north arrows and scale bars created distortions which ranged from displaying a faint glow to completely altering the 3D-modeled ship structure (Figure 1). The color of the water during the three field seasons also impacted data analysis and the overall aesthetic quality of the 3D models. A more in-depth color correction process in *Photoshop* would potentially solve these issues. To improve the contrast of the green, brown, and yellow orthophotos, each was converted to a black and white image. The new black and white images significantly enhanced the ability to compare them with unit drawings.

The 2016 discovery of Emanuel Point III offered a unique opportunity to simultaneously map the shipwreck with traditional and photogrammetric methods. The site offers better visibility than Emanuel Point II, a key impediment in previous photogrammetric testing.

FIGURE 1: Orthophoto of Emanuel Point II, unit 80N 505E demonstrating the glow created by presence of north arrow (Orthophoto created by author, 2016)

FIGURE 2: Orthophoto of Emanuel Point III test units (Orthophoto created by author 2016)

UWF archaeologists opened two test units in 2016 to map and adequately video the structure. The video resulted in a high-quality 3D model, which substantiated the need to continue photogrammetric procedures during subsequent excavations (Figure 2). The Emanuel Point III shipwreck discovery received high visibility within local and international press. Photogrammetric modeling of the site in coming years could certainly be utilized as a tool for public outreach programs as well as a tool for the long-term monitoring of the site.

Conclusions and Recommendations

Rapid advances in photography, computers, and photogrammetric software have changed the way underwater archaeologists document sites. Those acting as stewards of underwater cultural heritage must strive to always use the best methods at hand so that all potential data is gleaned from archaeological material. Excavations are inherently destructive, and thus portions of archaeological sites are commonly undisturbed so that future archaeologists may utilize more advanced methods and technology. The development of photogrammetric methods is a key illustration of the benefits of this mindset.

For the University of West Florida, the discovery of Emanuel Point III presents an opportunity to create standard operating procedures for photogrammetric methods. The methods and results presented here illustrate the initial photogrammetric testing of the Emanuel Point II and III shipwrecks. All resulting data is held at the University of West Florida Archaeology Institute and can be accessed by those interested in continuing photogrammetric testing. A future graduate student could write an entire master's thesis on the photogrammetry of the Emanuel Point shipwrecks. There is certainly potential to improve the methods described here during future excavations of Emanuel Point III. Some suggestions include collection of individual photographs taken by a high-resolution underwater camera, more in-depth color correction in *Photoshop*, and use of the best photogrammetric software package at the time. Advances in digital documentation methods will continue to expand underwater cultural heritage investigation techniques.

Acknowledgements

This study was funded in part by Florida Division of Historical Resources Special Category Grants. It was also supported by the University of West Florida Archaeology Institute and the Division of Anthropology and Archaeology. We would like to thank Stephen Atkinson, Charles Bendig, Meghan Memford, and Andrew Willard for allowing us to use their plan drawings and sketches for photogrammetric comparisons. Finally, this project would not have been possible without the early guidance of Kotaro Yamafune.

References

Aragón, Enrique, Sebastia Munar, Javier Rodríguez, and Kotaro Yamafune
2018 Underwater photogrammetric monitoring for mid-depth shipwrecks. *Journal of Cultural Heritage* 34: 255-260.

Atkinson, Stephen B.
2017 *Narrowed and Filled with Timber: An Analytical Study of the Aft Components of the Emanuel Point Two Shipwreck.* Master's Thesis. Department of Anthropology and Archaeology, University of West Florida, Pensacola, FL.

Balletti, Caterina, C. Beltrame, E. Costa, F. Guerra and P. Vernier
2015 Underwater Photogrammetry and 3D Reconstruction of Marble Cargos Shipwreck. *International Archives of the Photogrammetry, Remote Sensing & Spatial Information Sciences* Volume XL-5/W5.

Bendig, Charles D.
2016 *Studying the Hearts of Ships: 16th-century Mainmast Steps and Bilge Pumps Assemblies Through an Annales Nautical Archaeological Perspective.* Master's Thesis. Department of Anthropology and Archaeology, University of West Florida, Pensacola, FL.

Bratten, John R.
2012 The University of West Florida's Maritime Field School Experience. In *Global Perspectives on Archaeological Field Schools*, Harold Mytum, editor, pp. 147-164. Springer, New York, NY.

Burgess, Anthony
2013 *Underwater Aviation Archaeology: What is its Place and Value within Archaeology, and in Particular Maritime Archaeology?* Master's Thesis. University of Southampton, Southampton, U.K.

Drap, Pierre
2012 *Underwater Photogrammetry for Archaeology.* INTECH Open Access Publisher, Rijeka, Croatia.

McCarthy, John and Jonathan Benjamin
2014 Multi-image Photogrammetry for Underwater Arhaeological Site Recording: An Accessible, Diver-based Approach. *Journal of Maritime Archaeology* 9, 95-114.

SMITH, ROGER C., JAMES SPIREK, JOHN R. BRATTEN, AND DELLA A. SCOTT IRETON
1995   *The Emanuel Point Ships: Archaeological Investigations* 1992-1995. Bureau of Archaeological Research, Division of Historical Resources, Florida Department of State.

SMITH, ROGER C. (EDITOR)
2018a   *Florida's Lost Galleon: The Emanuel Point Shipwreck.* University Press of Florida, Gainesville, FL.

SMITH, ROGER C.
2018b   The Old Spaniard in *Florida's Lost Galleon: The Emanuel Point Shipwreck*, Roger C. Smith, editor, pp. 1-6. University Press of Florida, Gainesville, FL.

SOCIETY FOR HISTORICAL ARCHAEOLOGY
2016   Final Program of the 49th Annual Conference on Historical and Underwater Archaeology, January 6-9, Washington, D.C.

2017   Final Program of the 50th Annual Conference on Historical and Underwater Archaeology, January 4-8, Fort Worth, TX

VAN DAMME, THOMAS
2015   *Computer Vision Photogrammetry for Underwater Archaeological Site Recording in a Low-Visibility Environment. International Archives of the Photogrammetry, Remote Sensing & Spatial Information Sciences* Volume XL-5/W5.

WORTH, JOHN E.
2018   *Florida's Forgotten Colony in Florida's Lost Galleon: The Emanuel Point Shipwreck*, Roger C. Smith, editor, pp. 34-67. University Press of Florida, Gainesville, FL.

YAMAFUNE, KOTARO
2016   *Using Computer Vision Photogrammetry (Agisoft Photoscan) to Record and Analyze Underwater Shipwreck Sites.* Doctoral Dissertation. Department of Anthropology, Texas A&M University, College Station, TX.

• • • • • • • • • • • • • • • •

Micah B. Minnocci
The Division of Anthropology and Archaeology
University of West Florida
11000 University Parkway
Pensacola, FL 32514
(321) 288-6767
mm190@students.uwf.edu

Hunter W. Whitehead
The Division of Anthropology and Archaeology
University of West Florida
11000 University Parkway
Pensacola, FL 32514
(850) 368-2591
h.w.whitehead3@gmail.com

Rebuilding the Past: Digitizing Ship Lines into 3D Models

Arik J. K. Bord

In its continuing effort to "standardize the publication of shipbuilding data," the J. Richard Steffy Ship Reconstruction Laboratory at Texas A&M University has continually been looking at better and more efficient ways to digitize the vast library of ship lines plans it has accumulated in the lab's 30+ year history. This paper briefly looks at several dedicated ship design software packages and provides a methodology and workflow for digitizing lines drawings into 3D models.

Introduction

In its continuing effort to "standardize the publication of shipbuilding data," the J. Richard Steffy Ship Reconstruction Laboratory at Texas A&M University (colloquially referred to as the ShipLab) has continually been looking at better and more efficient ways to digitize the vast library of ship lines plans it has accumulated in the lab's 30+ year history (Castro et al. 2018). Additionally, the presence of 3D modeling and virtual reconstructions of ships poses opportunities for even greater precision and accuracy in ship reconstruction methodologies (Dostal and Yamafune 2018). Different software packages have been used in recent years to assist the maritime archaeologist reconstruct ships and ship construction, including *Rhino, Photoscan, Maya,* etc. (Hazlet 2007). In an effort to explore a more streamlined methodology to import and digitize existing lines drawings, three dedicated ship design programs were evaluated to determine the ease and precision of creating a 3D hull-form from a scanned set of lines and develop a procedural workflow of the digitization process for use in the ShipLab.

Software

A number of criteria were established for identification of software programs for this project. Those criteria included that software programs be open source or freeware, have an intuitive and customizable graphical user interface (GUI), have the ability to be exported into standard 3D formats, and have built-in hydrostatic calculation capabilities. Three dedicated ship design software programs were identified meeting these criteria. ShipShape is design software created by the Wolfson Unit associated with the University of Southampton. It is designed to work with their suite of proprietary ship design and hydrostatic software packages, but does contain some built-in hydrostatic calculations. Due to time constraints, this program was not explored fully, however the author's initial impression was that the GUI was markedly less user friendly than the other two software packages tested. The next program, called *FREE!ship*, was an open-source program. Although it was officially discontinued in 2007, it is still available to download. As it hasn't been updated in several years, its user interface is somewhat outdated and less intuitive. The third and best option evaluated, DELFTship, was created by the original developer of *FREE!ship*. Developed in association with the Delft University of Technology, *DELFTship* uses much the same base code as *FREE!ship* (Engeland 2007). It has a modern, intuitive user interface and is updatable and upgradable. There are free and paid versions of DELFTship. The free version is functionally a lot like *FREE!ship* but with a few new features and a better GUI, while the paid version includes some additional template models and hydrostatic calculations. After evaluating all three programs, the decision was ultimately made to develop a procedure for lines plan digitization using DELFTship. A tentative set of *Santa Catarina do Monte Sinai's* lines were chosen as the test subject to develop the procedure.

Ship Lines Plans

The first known set of ship lines drawings come from Baker [1589] and they have been a regular and necessary feature of naval architecture since the early 17th century (Hamilton 1977). A lines plan drawing is a diagram that describes the three-dimensional shape of the hull and is a fundamental tool used to understand a ship's design and reconstruction (Steffy, 1994). From a lines plan, the nautical archaeologist can calculate hydrostatic information, infer a ship's sailing characteristics, and visualize the compound curves which make up the submerged portions of a ship's hull. Lines plans consist of three drawings demonstrating the shape of the interior surface of the hull planking of a ship. Similar to modern blueprints or structure architectural drawings, each line on a ship lines plan represents the intersection of the ship's hull along specified planes running vertically, transverse, and horizontally to the keel (buttock lines, stations, and waterlines, respectively) (Steffy 1994). Using lines plans enable ship architects and nautical archaeologists to visualize a three-dimensional shape of a hull in a two-dimensional format.

Santa Catarina do Monte Sinai

A lines plan which was originally generated as a class project for *The Research and Reconstruction of Ships* course at Texas A&M University was used as a test subject to determine the utility of the *DELFTship* software. The original course project examined the feasibility and methodology for determining ship construction and hull characteristics from iconography. At the completion of the project a theoretical reconstruction of *Santa Catarina do Monte Sinai* was produced, including a lines plan. This ship is believed to be the one depicted in the painting entitled *Portuguese Carracks off a Rocky Coast*, located in the National Maritime Museum, Greenwich, London (Figure 1). This ship was chosen as a test-case for use in *DELFTship* because of the author's prior knowledge of its history and its reconstructed measurements for the hull curves in the creation of the lines drawings.

The Iconography

Portuguese Carracks off a Rocky Coast is believed to portray the arrival of *Infanta Dona Beatriz* of Portugal on *Santa Catarina* just prior to her wedding with the Duke of Savoy in 1521 (Matos 2005). The painting is highly detailed and is depicted in the Flemish style popularized in the 16th Century. In fact, this particular piece is likely the oldest known example of Flemish-style non-religious maritime artwork (Royal Museums Greenwich 2015).

While disputed, some scholars believe that the depiction in the painting is of the same ship in several angles (Matos 2005; Barker 2003). Assuming that this is true, the various "views" of the ship can be combined to create an animation and determine various construction features of the vessel.

The Ship

Santa Catarina was built in Cochim, India and commissioned in 1517. It displaced about 700-800 toneis (approximately 1190-1760 metric tonnes), which made it a very large ship for the time (Barker 2003; Castro 2008). By 1521 it had completed two voyages to Lisbon and had earned a reputation as being the most powerful Indiaman of the fleet (Barker 2003). Like other Portuguese *naus* of the period, it was designed to carry the relatively large volume, low weight, cargo of pepper (Hazlett 2007).

FIGURE 1: Portuguese Carracks off a Rocky Coast. Painting ca. 1540, artist unknown. Image from Wikimedia Commons.

In preparation for its mission to transport the 20 year old second daughter of King Manuel I to her wedding with Charles III of Savoy, many modifications to the inside of the ship are said to have been made: spiral staircases in the sterncastle led to new cabins in the lower decks, galleries were added for the crew to reach the helm without disturbing the betrothed or her entourage, the half deck was covered with a gilded canopy to serve as the nobles' mess and reception hall, a bridge was built from the staircase leading to the half deck, over the boats to the bulwark, to serve as a gangway for the aristocracy, and more guns were added to protect the union, which was already four years in the making (Barker 2003). In turn, these modifications required the capstan be moved as well. Because of these modifications, *Santa Catarina* would later be used as a flagship for voyages to and from India twice more before it was lost in 1525 (Barker 2003).

In all likelihood, *Santa Catarina* sank during a storm in the South Atlantic, but for the next decade, rumors were spread about the fate of the ship. The most prolific of the rumors was that the ship had been besieged and pillaged by French pirates off the coast of Portugal, and that all hands were slaughtered before the ship was scuttled. In 1536 supposed evidence was discovered linking a specific pirate to the ship's demise, however, no letters of marque or any documentation have been found which substantiate the rumors. Still, several skirmishes and incidents occurred between French and Portuguese fleets in the name of *Santa Catarina* (Barker 2003).

Initial Reconstruction and Generation of Lines Plan

The lower hull shape and proportions of the *Santa Catarina* reconstruction were based largely on that of the Pepper Wreck, a Portuguese nau excavated and analyzed by the ShipLab; the reconstruction of which has drastically increased our understanding of Iberian shipbuilding tradition (Castro 2005; Castro and Fonseca 2015). Various changes were made to the reconstructed Pepper Wreck lower hull design to incorporate knowledge learned about the proportions of Portuguese *naus* since the initial project was completed and other inconstancies with Castro's (2005) design. The main changes made were to fair the sheer, widen the midship bottom flat to one-half of the maximum breadth, and slightly lengthen the stem and sternpost (partly due to the faired sheer, partly to better fit the profile of the hull). Taking the measure of 40.25 m between posts for the sheer (using the proportions of the Pepper Wreck, scaled to the known tonnage of *Santa Catarina*), the broadside view of the ship from the painting was printed to scale (the scale used for the drawing was 1:100). The arc of the bow and angle of the sternpost were traced and projected downward to determine the location of the keel to 9.65 m below the midship sheer (assuming the ship in the painting was ballasted at its loaded waterline and that waterline was 3/5 total height at midships). The keel and posts were then projected and laid out accordingly.

Using *DELFTship* to digitize Ship Lines

A few different methods can be used to digitize lines using the *DELFTship* software. A model can be produced by simply "tracing" the lines with the edges of the control net after the existing lines drawings are positioned as a background image. After some experimentation, it was determined the most efficient and accurate way to digitize the lines was to enter the control point coordinates directly by using hand measurements from the original lines and converting them to 1:1 scale. Measurements can be taken off the original paper lines using dividers or rulers, or by setting the scale and using the measuring tool in *Photoshop*. Using the latter option, the (x, y, z) coordinates were measured from the reconstruction of *Santa Catarina* and entered into the program. The (0,0,0) point in the virtual environment is the point where a line projected downward from the interior surface of the sternpost at the centerline meets the baseline drawn at the rabbet of the keel (*DELFTship* Marine Software 2018).

Setup of the template hull model

Opening a new project requires setting overall dimensions and beginning control points in the model. *DELFTship* automatically provides a basic hull template, including a control net, to use as a starting point; variables such as length, breadth, draft, and initial number of control points in the control net can be input. The program sets the midship position by default and allows the user to choose the number of control points in the vertical plane, as well as forward and aft of the midships point.

The initial control points were kept at a minimum in order to maintain control of the hull curves and control net matrix. Therefore, two vertical, two fore, and three aft points were set in the blank hull. The extra aft point became the lower end of the sternpost at the keel level, and the aftermost lower point on the template hull-form became the point where the fashion pieces meet the post. This point is often referred to as the height of the runs. The length and beam were set at a 1:1 scale (40.25 m and 13.2 m, respectively). *DELFTship* sets the overall height of the model at 4-times the entered draft. Setting the draft at 3.5 m made the height of the virtual environment approximately 13.5 m. The draft level was changed later in the project settings to reflect the actual loaded waterline of 6.25 m (3/5 of the height of the sheer at the midship frame).

Once the project was started, a scanned copy of the drawn lines plan was imported, set as a "background image," and scaled to 1:1 in the virtual environment. *DELFTship* is able to import .png or .jpg files. Three

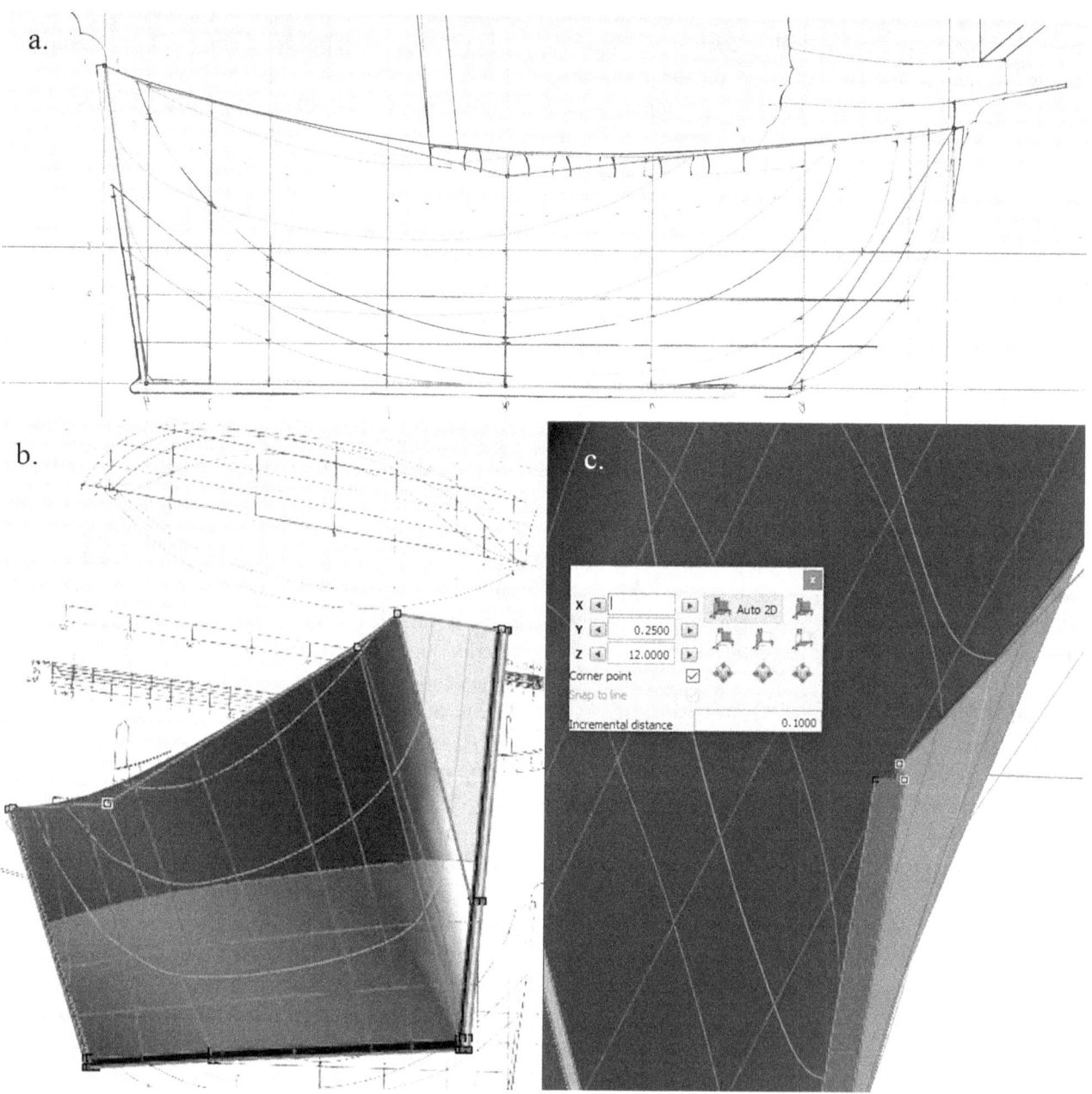

FIGURE 2: (a) The blank hull and background images appropriately scaled and laid out; (b) The extruded sternpost allows for more accurate lines and hydrostatic calculations; (c) Setting the top of the stem offset. After the hull centerline is shifted and the keel and post placeholders are extruded, the upper coordinates of the sheer and posts should be changed to accurately account for displacement or dimensional differences along the length of the posts. On the *Santa Catarina do Monte Sinai* reconstruction, the stem is molded 0.3 m at the keel and 0.25 m at the sheer. Therefore, the control points at the top of the stem were readjusted from 0.3 m (y-axis) to 0.25.

copies of the scanned image needed to be imported and scaled to the project. On each imported image, scale was set by aligning the (0,0,0) point on each respective elevation view of the lines drawing with the (0,0,0) point in virtual space, selecting a point on the imported image which have known coordinates, and entering those coordinates at that point. This automatically aligns and scales the image to the anchor point of (0,0,0) and the point selected for scaling. For better accuracy, all three images were scaled to the sheer (profile) view and the point selected was at the furthest extent from the origin: the inner stem at the sheer, which on *Santa Catarina* is located at (x, y, z) coordinates (40.25, 0, 12 m). Once the scale was set, each image was switched to their respective views and realigned to that particular view's (0,0) point and the origin point in the virtual environment. Once scaled and positioned, the background images were exported into *DELFTship*'s proprietary background image format, which preserves the scaling and position data for use in future projects.

Next, the control points on the initial hull template were moved to set the height of the sheer at the stem, sternpost, after-most station, and amidships, all from the sheer view. Also, all points along the baseline were set at the keel rabbet, including the base of the sternpost, amidships, and the stem (Figure 2a). The extra point on the aft-sheer became the sheer point of the aftermost station.

The next procedure was to reenter the project settings and set references for the stations, waterlines, and buttock lines (in *DELFTship*, stations are entered in meters along the x axis from the origin, buttock lines along the y axis from the centerline, and the waterlines along the z axis from the baseline). Some of the variables needed for hydrostatic calculations, including the midships location, draft, and thickness of the planking were also entered. Doing this before the hull shape was formed made visualization easier as the model was shaped.

Before inserting hull lines, the dimensions of the keel and posts must be accounted for in the model. The centerline along the keel and posts were offset and the edges of each extruded and lofted to create a rough shape matching the full sided and 1/2 the moulded dimensions of the keel and posts. *Santa Catarina*'s keel is moulded to 0.6 m and sided to 0.4 m, so the placeholder keel was extruded to -0.4 m (z axis) and -0.3 m (y axis), the top of the stem to 0.45 m (x axis) and -0.3 m (y axis), and the sternpost to -0.3 m (both x and y axes), respectively (extruding edges are directional, therefore negative numbers are used to indicate the direction of extrusion from the origin) (Figure 2b). After extruding the posts, the points at the top of the stem were adjusted to reflect the taper of the moulded stem from 0.3 m at the keel to 0.25 m at the sheer (Figure 2c).

Digitization of the Lines and Creation and Fairing the Model

In *DELFTship*, the Plane tool essentially slices the model's control net and inserts control points wherever the plane intersects an existing edge. This was used to insert stations, buttock lines and waterlines, and form the shape of the hull. Transverse planes were inserted for all stations and the new control points were adjusted to their respective coordinates on the lines drawing (e.g. a plane was inserted for station 3 at 5.1 m and the point inserted by the plane at the sheer was adjusted along the y and z axes to match the breadth and height of the sheer at section 3, respectively) (Figure 3a). This procedure was repeated for the buttock lines and waterlines (vertical planes for buttock lines, horizontal for waterlines). Again, as a line was inserted, each new point was repositioned to its respective three-dimensional coordinates.

DELFTship offers several textures to visualize the fairness of the model. Once the lines were inserted into the model and the general shape was set, the control points were tweaked and manipulated to fair the shape (Figure 3b). Any creases, bulges, or wavy surfaces could be seen using the zebra stripes or one of the textures available on the environment map selection of the GUI. Some points needed to be added by splitting an edge to fine tune

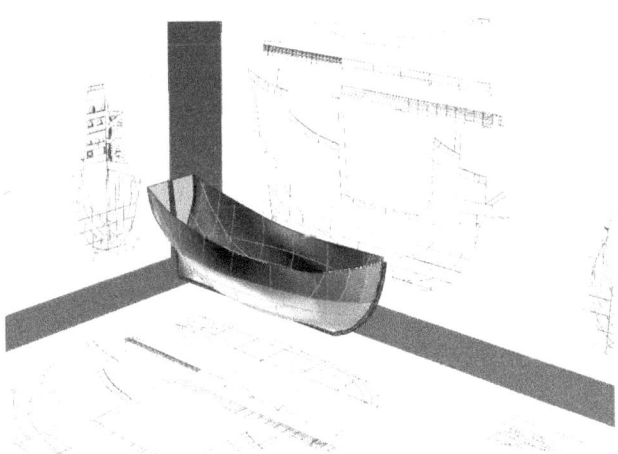

FIGURE 3: (a) Insert sections, buttock lines, and waterlines using the plane tool. Make sure the box Do not move surrounding points is checked; (b) The environment map offers several different metalized textures to help visualize the fairness of the model.

a curve and some control points needed to be shifted around until the shape was properly faired.

Final Steps

Once faired using the basic control net, the mesh was subdivided three times to smooth the curves. This process splits each segment of the control mesh to create more control points. More control points create smoother compound curves in the model. Once subdivided, fairness should be checked again, as any creases or bulges will be amplified by the subdivision procedure. Finally, hydrostatic calculations were run and the final model was exported as a stereo-lithography (.stl) file for future manipulation in *Rhino* (Figure 4).

One of the features built-in to *DELFTship* is the ability to perform various hydrostatic calculations, including intact stability, hull resistance, center of buoyancy, block and prismatic coefficients, and displacement information. The paid version of *DELFTship* offers some additional hydrostatic formulae, but most of those are geared toward modern commercial vessels and don't apply to historic wooden sailing ships.

The final hull shape can be exported in various 2D and 3D formats, including waveform (.obj) or stereo-lithography (.stl) files. These files can then be imported into another program such as *Rhino* or *Maya* to build the rest of the castles and quickwork, add planking around the hull shape, and complete the digital reconstruction of the ship for analysis, visualization, etc. Upper hull elements can be created within *DELFTship* itself, but other programs like *Rhino* or *Maya* are better suited, in this author's opinion, for plank-by-plank ship reconstruction, as was done by Hazlet (2007).

Conclusion

The purpose of this project was to develop a procedure for digitizing existing ship lines plans for more accurate visualization and hydrostatic calculations on vessels from the historical and archaeological record. The *DELFTship* software was found to be easy to use and a very useful and powerful tool. The use of this software can greatly increase the ease and accuracy of ship reconstruction and analysis. Additionally, extruding additional surfaces across the top edges of the model would allow it to be 3D printed at any scale for water tank testing, physical model building, and other visualization, educational, and testing methods for use in museums or other public outreach programs, academic study, etc. At the time of this writing, a plan is underway to apply this workflow to the process of digitizing and publishing the ShipLab's massive archival collection of inked and penciled paper lines plans, ship reconstructions, and treatise analyses. The digitization of the collection could unlock the possibility of new analyses and research projects for current and future Shiplab personnel and students trying to further their understanding of shipbuilding traditions, historic globalization through shipping, and the culture contact which accompanies those phenomena.

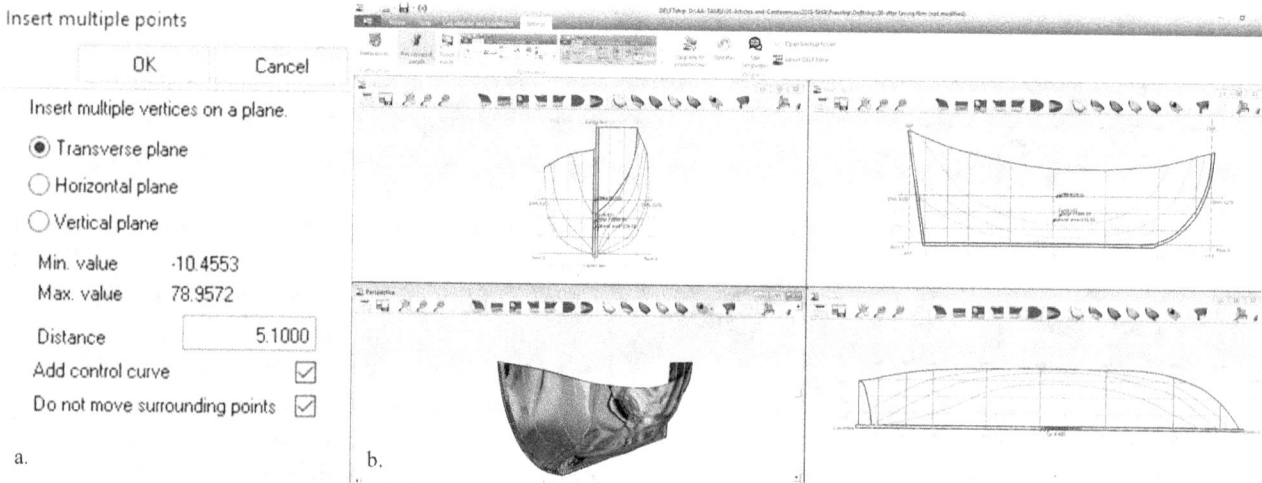

FIGURE 4: Final lower hull model of the reconstructed Portuguese Indiaman *Santa Catarina do Monte Sinai* with lines drawings projected behind. This model was exported as a stereo-lithography (.stl) file for import into *Rhino* for further reconstruction.

Acknowledgments

This paper was originally presented at the 2019 Society for Historical Archaeology Conference in a symposium exhibiting ongoing research projects at the J. Richard Steffy Ship Reconstruction Laboratory, colloquially referred to as the ShipLab. I would like to thank Dr. Filipe Castro and some of my colleagues in the ShipLab for their support in organizing the symposium, and also their encouragement to participate in the symposium and prepare this manuscript: Marijo Guthier-Bérubé, Charles Bendig, Ricardo Borrero, and Joshua Farrar.

References

BAKER, M.
[1589]   Fragments of Ancient English Shipwrightry. Cambridge: Pepys Library. MS 2820.

BARKER, RICHARD
2003   Showing the Flag in 1521: Wafting Beatriz to Savoy. *Presented at the joint XI Reunião Internacional da História da Náutica e da Hidrografia and VIII Jornadas de História Iber-Americana (2002).* Portimão, Portugal. Richard Barker, translator. Richard Barker-Water Engineer, personal webpage, Last accessed November 28, 2015 <http://home.clara.net/rabarker/Showing-the-flag-web.htm>.

CASTRO, FILIPE VIERA DE
2005   *The Pepper Wreck: A Portuguese Indiaman at the Mouth of the Tagus River.* Texas A&M University Press. College Station, Texas.

CASTRO, FILIPE VIERA DE
2008   In Search of Unique Iberian Ship Design Concepts. *Historical Archaeology.* 42(2):63-87.

CASTRO, FILIPE, CHARLES BENDIG, MARIJO BÉRUBÉ, RICARDO BORRERO, NICOLAS BUDSBERG, CHRISTOPHER DOSTAL, A. MONTEIRO, C. SMITH, R. TORRES, AND KOTARO YAMAFUNE
2018   Recording, Publishing, and Reconstructing Wooden Shipwrecks. *Journal of Maritime Archaeology.* 13(1):55-66.

CASTRO, FILIPE VIERA DE AND NUNO FONSECA
2015   The Pepper Wreck as a Case Study for the Portuguese India Route Ships. In *Shipwrecks Around the World: Revelations of the Past,* Sila Tripati, editor, pp. 1-25. Delta Book World, New Delhi, India.

DELFTSHIP MARINE SOFTWARE
2018   *DELFTship Manual.* Hoofddorp, Netherlands Dostal, Christopher and Kotaro Yamafune

2018   Photogrammetric Texture Mapping: A Method for Increasing the Fidelity of 3D Models of Cultural Heritage Materials. *Journal of Archaeological Science: Reports.* 18:430-436 Engeland, M. v. (Martijn_vE) <info@DELFTship.net>

2007   *FREE!ship continues as DELFTship.* BoatDesign.net discussion board, p2., January 29 (posted date), >https://www.boatdesign.net/threads/free-ship-continues-as-DELFTship.15607/page-2>.

HAMILTON, RICK
1977   A History of Naval Architecture 1400-1850. Texas A&M Nautical Archaeology Program Library Offprints. College Station, Texas.

HAZLETT, A. D.
2007   *The Nau of the Livro Nautico: Reconstructing a Sixteenth-Century Indiaman from Texts.* Doctoral Dissertation, Department of Anthropology, Texas A&M University.

MATOS, LUÍS JORGE
2005   *Velas e Manobras.* unpublished manuscript.

ROYAL MUSEUMS GREENWICH
[1540]   *Portuguese Carracks off a Rocky Coast.* Catalog No. BHC0705. Last accessed November 28, 2015 <http://collections.rmg.co.uk/collections/objects/12197.html>.

STEFFY, J. RICHARD
1994   *Wooden ship building and the interpretation of shipwrecks.* 1st ed. Texas A&M University Press. College Station, Texas.

. . . .

Arik J. K. Bord
Department of Anthropology
Texas A&M University
Anthropology
TAMU 4352
College Station, TX 77843-4352
(530) 518-7170
arik.bord@tamu.edu

Identifying Aircraft Artifacts Ex Situ: The Life History of an F4U Corsair

Hunter W. Whitehead

In 2016, representatives of Saiki, Japan presented an historical aircraft engine, propeller, and partial wing to the Naval History and Heritage Command (NHHC). The artifacts were discovered by accident some years prior when fishermen caught their nets on a submerged U.S. naval aircraft in Saiki Bay. Residents of the city of Saiki attempted to raise the aircraft but were only able to recover it in part. Having little archaeological context, NHHC researchers are tasked with identifying the artifacts and defining the wartime actions that resulted in aircraft losses in the area of Saiki.

Introduction

In March of 2016, the Naval History and Heritage Command (NHHC) received an aircraft engine with attached propeller, and a partial wing from representatives of Saiki, Japan, located on the island of Kyushu. Several years earlier, a Japanese fisherman caught the engine and propeller in fishing nets; subsequently, Saiki locals attempted to raise the rest of the submerged vessel. Failing at this endeavor, the few aircraft components ended up on display at Saiki's Yawaragi Peace Memorial Hall in 2007. Saiki residents' initial historical research led them to believe the components are associated with an F4U-1D Corsair attached to the USS *Intrepid* (CV11). In 2015, they contacted curators at the *Intrepid* Sea, Air and Space Museum, whom directed their efforts to the NHHC (Naval History and Heritage Command 2016), as managers of the U.S. Navy's sunken military craft.

Archaeologists and conservators with the NHHC Underwater Archaeology Branch developed an initial documentation and conservation plan upon receiving the artifacts. The aircraft components have little archaeological context; however, they retain emotional value. There is meaning behind these artifacts that not only tell the story of the men and women who dedicated their lives to the protection of their country but also about a larger struggle. Below are the initial research steps taken by the author as part of an NHHC internship to confirm the identity of the aircraft components and create a timeline of events during which the wreck may have occurred.

1. Analyze the diagnostic features of the physical artifacts to help identify the aircraft type.
2. Utilize information discovered about the aircraft type to define the timeline of wartime action, which included the type(s) of aircraft in the area of interest (i.e. Kyushu region).
3. Extract a list of Bureau Numbers (BuNos) belonging to the relevant aircraft type(s) lost during military engagements in the area of interest.

Analysis of Aircraft Components

As subsequent research tasks were driven by identification of possible aircraft type(s), research began with the artifacts themselves. Researchers obtained scanned copies of the engine, wing, and propeller parts manuals for the F4U-1D Corsair from the Steven F. Udvar-Hazy National Air and Space Museum Archives (Chief of Bureau of Aeronautics 1943, 1945, 1946). Assessments made between these manuals and the aircraft components revealed major similarities and indicated that the artifacts were prospective components of an F4U Corsair (Figure 1). The following is a comprehensive analysis of each aircraft component.

FIGURE 1: F4U Corsair with wings folded for storage (Courtesy of NHHC Archives, 80-G-425527)

Engine Analysis

Preliminary observations of the remaining engine components, primarily the propeller shaft, partial cam, pistons, rods, crank shaft, and cylinders narrowed its identification to two possible models (Figure 2). The R-2800 was the first and only 18-cylinder twin radial developed and manufactured in quantity by Pratt & Whitney (White 2001). Pratt & Whitney began manufacturing the R-2800 engine in 1939, providing a *terminus post quem* of the aircraft engine type (White 2001). It appears that the only other 18-cylinder twin radial engine produced in quantity during this period was the Wright R-3350 Duplex-Cyclone which upon initial observation is markedly different than that of the R-2800. The two engines have different cylinder bore and stroke sizes. The R-2800 has a cylinder bore of 5 and 3/4" and stroke of 6" (White 2001), while the R-3350 has a cylinder bore of 6 and 1/8" and stroke of 6 and 5/16" (White 1995). The measurements of the aircraft engine cylinders closely matched that of the R-2800.

FIGURE 2: Aircraft engine attached to bent propeller (Photo taken by author 2016)

Upon prospective identification of the engine as an R-2800, researchers then considered the five variations of the engine which appear to contain the same basic components with minor discrepancies. Researchers examined the parts manual containing the R-2800-8, -8w, -10, -10w, and -65 (Chief of Bureau of Aeronautics 1944). After consideration, the following components may have indicated these specific variations: reduction gear housing, accessory drives, distributor adapter, magneto adapter and propeller thrust bearing, oil scavenge pump, reduction drive and propeller shaft, support plates, and crank case. Unfortunately, these components are missing from the engine or are so badly degraded that identification between such minor discrepancies is unlikely. Furthermore, the parts manual is vague when discussing the parts' differences, i.e., Part X used instead of Part Y. Without a working knowledge of these minor parts differences, or a detailed parts catalog with schematics, variation identification is doubtful. Fortunately, the only R-2800 bearing aircraft that operated in Kyushu were the F6F Hellcat and the F4U Corsair (Office of Naval Records and Library 1945t).

Wing Piece Analysis

The wing piece contains the center section where the landing gear is located (Figure 3). It is likely the forward section of the port wing, missing a large portion of the aft. What remains of the wing section are the ribs, aluminum cover around the ribs, landing gear, and hydraulic systems for both the bending wing and landing gear. The wing piece was, upon first observations, very indicative of an F4U Corsair, as the bend in the wing is a distinctive trait among World War II era aircraft. Other initial observations revealed fully retractable landing gear, hydraulic systems for both the landing gear door and the folding wing. Upon initial assessments with the F4U Corsair parts manual, it was clear that the wing

FIGURE 3: Wing section with attached landing gear components (Photo taken by author 2016)

piece has identical components.

Some preliminary archival research revealed what types of aircraft each Task Group utilized in the area during the pertinent timeline. These aircraft are listed as: F6F Hellcats, F4U Corsairs, SB2C Helldivers, TBM Avengers, 0S2U Kingfishers, and FM Wildcats (Office of Naval Records and Library 1945t). Of these aircraft, only the F4U Corsair and F6F Hellcat have variations of the Pratt & Whitney R-2800 engine. They are also the only types that contain similar folding wings, and fully retractable landing gear. Thus, determining the differences between these two aircraft and their hydraulics, landing gear, and wing systems became a key focus of the project.

Another visit to the Udvar-Hazy Air and Space Museum's Archives exposed the stark differences between the two aircraft very quickly. The F6F Hellcat and F4U Corsair both have wings that fold for storage, though do so in dissimilar ways. The F6F Hellcat wings pivot up and toward the aft of the plane, somewhat like a bird's wings. The F4U Corsair wings simply folds upward toward the fuselage. Each aircraft's parts manual showed in detail the hydraulics system involved in these processes (Chief of Bureau of Aeronautics 1945, 1947). The F6F has a wing hydraulics component that is horizontal and closer to the fuselage, compared to the F4U's components on the farther side of the wing, opposite the fuselage. The hydraulics systems are both in completely dissimilar places within the wing. Comparably, the landing gear's hydraulics for the F4U and F6F Hellcat are vastly different. The wing piece is in fact that of an F4U Corsair. This postulate is based on visual observations of the wing curvature, hydraulics systems, and landing gear.

Propeller Analysis

It appears that most components of the propeller are present. The de-icing unit is not visible because it is inside the hub section, though parts of the dome, hub, blades, and distributor remain. One of the three blades is missing a significant portion, and all three are bent. The fact that three blades are present rejects the possibility that the engine is part of an F4U-4 Corsair, which has four propeller blades. According to the F4U Corsair parts manual, the propeller used was a Hamilton Standard with a hub number of 23E50 and blade number 6443A-21 (Chief of Bureau of Aeronautics 1945). The F6F Hellcat parts manual also lists a Hamilton Standard Propeller with a hub number of 23E50 with blade numbers 6501A or 6541A (Chief of Bureau of Aeronautics 1947). The propeller diameter of the F6F Hellcat (13 feet 1 inch) and F4U Corsair (13 feet 4 inch) are different, and it was hoped that these differences would assist in engine and propeller type determination (Chief of Bureau of Aeronautics 1945, 1947). Unfortunately, the blades are far too damaged to obtain an accurate propeller diameter. Also, the individual blade measurements were not included in the parts manuals, which could have helped to determine the propeller type.

Without easy access to an F6F Hellcat or F4U Corsair, blade measurements were taken by Michael Boitnott of the National Naval Aviation Museum in Pensacola, Florida from an FG-1D and a F6F-3. It should be noted here that the FG-1D Corsair is an F4U Corsair that was made by Goodyear Aircraft Company. During World War II, the U.S. Navy requested more Corsairs than Vought Aircraft Industries could supply. To meet this demand, Vought was required to outsource production of its F4U Corsair to Goodyear Aircraft Company as an FG designation, and Brewster Aeronautical Corporation as an F3A designation. These designations are solely to define the manufacturer, while the aircraft itself is manufactured the same way (Tillman 1979:7).

The blade measurement of the FG-1D is 71 and 11/16 inches. The blade measurement of the F6F-3 is 71 and 3/16 inches. Being exactly a 1/2-inch difference, the probability that the difference could be determined on the degraded blades was drastically reduced. In this case, the two complete blades had measurements of 70 and 3/8 inches, significantly shorter than the hard measurements taken by Boitnott. The dissimilarities may be attributed to degradation, the angle of the damaged propeller blades, or even the result of human error on the behalf of either Boitnott or the researchers taking measurements. There are serial numbers on the hub of each blade that are plausibly still present. Therefore, if one were so inclined, the blades may be disassembled to possibly discover the propeller's identity. Unfortunately, the propeller and engine did not reveal a specific aircraft type, and only with archival research was a set of possibilities refined. The wing piece is more conclusively part of an F4U Corsair, and only by association can the engine and propeller be considered.

Analysis of Archival Documents

To understand a very complex series of assaults during the Pacific Campaigns of WWII, researchers implemented a systematic survey of archival documents. By beginning with a very broad scope, they determined the specific Task Forces, Task Groups, aircraft carriers, and air groups involved with the Kyushu region. As a precursor to this analysis, a brief history of the WWII Pacific Campaign, as related to the assaults on Kyushu is considered.

Brief History of the Later Years of the WWII Pacific Campaign

Late in the WWII Pacific Campaign, 1944, it was obvious to naval fleet coordinators that a direct assault on the Japanese home islands would be necessary for victory. Okinawa, only 350 miles from Kyushu, the southernmost home island of Japan, was to become the warehouse for the assault (Astor 1995). As part of a broad strategy for the invasion of Okinawa, called Operation Iceberg, the U.S. Navy executed simultaneous air attacks on Okinawa and airfields of Kyushu (Figure 4). These attacks began in March 1945 and continued during occupation. The initial and steady attacks of Kyushu were operated in direct support of the invasion and occupation of Okinawa.

The following analysis is broken into two separate timetables: Task Force 58 and Task Force 38. The initial assault of American Naval forces on Kyushu occurred in March 1945 by the Pacific Fifth Fleet's Task Force (TF) 58 under the command of Vice-Admiral Marc A. Mitscher (Chief of Bureau of Aeronautics 1945s, 1945t). By the end of May 1945, the Fifth Fleet was reorganized as the Pacific Third Fleet. As per this reorganization, TF 58 became TF 38, and Mitshcer was relieved by Vice-Admiral John McCain (Sherman 1950). Only events that affected the area of interest, Kyushu, are included in the analysis.

Task Force 58

TF 58, operating under the Pacific Fifth Fleet, consisted of four Task Groups (TG): 58.1, 58.2, 58.3, and 58.4 (Office of Naval Records and Library 1945c). Each TG consisted of various ships and aircraft carriers. Table 1 illustrates the TG that each carrier is associated with during the period of 14 March to 28 May 1945. The TF 58 Action Reports, from which these data were discovered, also includes a general timeline of strikes, sorties, and movements of the fleet (Office of Naval Records and Library 1945c, 1945d, 1945e, 1945g, 1945h, 1945i, 1945j, 1945k, 1945l, 1945m, 1945n, 1945o, 1945q, 1945t, 1945v, 1945w). Major strikes against Kyushu during TF 58's period of operations are included. It should be noted that it is possible that minor strikes or sorties on Kyushu may have been excluded from these broad Action Reports, and specific documentary evidence would help elucidate the full extent of U.S. naval action.

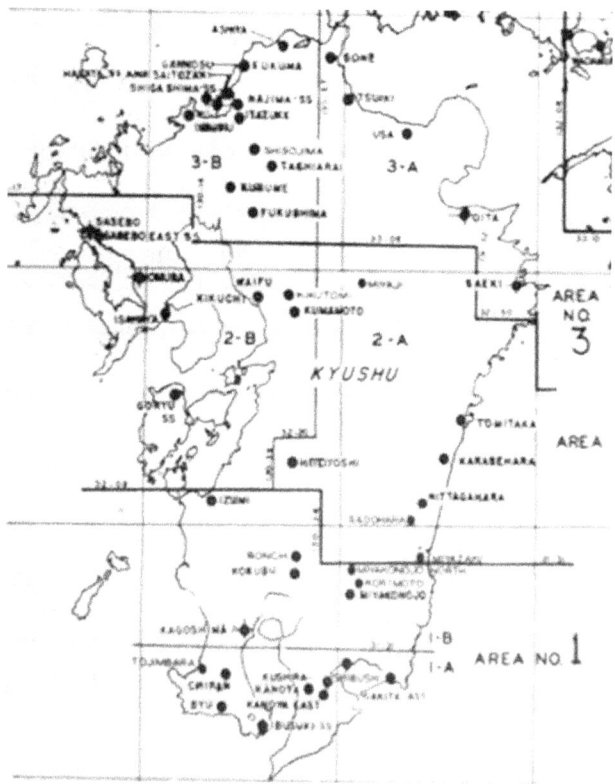

FIGURE 4: Task Group Target Areas (Office of Naval Records and Library 1945t)

Task Group 58.1	Task Group 58.2	Task Group 58.3	Task Group 58.4
Hornet (CV12)	Franklin (CV13)	Essex (CV9)	Yorktown (CV10)
Bennington (CV20)	Hancock (CV19)	Bunker Hill (CV17)	Intrepid (CV11)
Wasp (CV18)	San Jacinto (CVL30)	Cabot (CVL28)	Enterprise (CV6)
Belleau Wood (CVL24)	Bataan (CVL29)	Monterey (CVL26)	Langley (CVL27)
			Independence (CVL22)

TABLE 1: TF 58 aircraft carrier organization during period of 14 March - 28 May 1945 (Office of Naval Records and Library 1945)

Task Group 38.1	Task Group 38.3	Task Group 38.4
Bennington (CV20)	Randolph (CV15)	Yorktown (CV10)
Lexington (CV16)	Essex (CV9)	Shangri-La (CV38)
Hancock (CV19)	Ticonderoga (CV14)	Wasp (CV18)
San Jacinto (CVL30)	Monterey (CVL26)	Bon Homme Richard (CV31)
Belleau Wood (CVL24)	Bataan (CVL29)	Independence (CVL22)

TABLE 2: TF 38 aircraft carrier organization during 1945 (Office of Naval Records and Library 1945s)

Task Force 38

TF 38, operating under the freshly reorganized Pacific Third Fleet, consisted of three TG: 38.1, 38.3, and 38.4 (Office of Naval Records and Library 1945a). This TF operated from the reorganization, May 28, until the end of the war. Table 2 illustrates the various aircraft carriers attached to each TG. Unfortunately, compared to TF 58, the documentary evidence of TF 38 is sparse (Office of Naval Records and Library 1945a, 1945d, 1945e, 1945f, 1945j, 1945k, 1945m, 1945o, 1945p, 1945q, 1945r, 1945u, 1945v, 1945w.) The force was certainly still sending strikes and sorties to Kyushu's airfields, primarily the main airfield of Kanoya. The TF's principal focus appears to have been supporting the ongoing invasion strategy of Okinawa. They did so by flying Combat Air Patrols protecting the land forces from aerial attacks incoming from Japan's main island, Honshu. Most strikes during the latter period of the war appear to have been targeted at Honshu and surrounding islands, but occasional strikes against Kyushu occurred.

Naval Aircraft Accident Reports

Researchers determined that it would be necessary to refer to individual aircraft carrier Action Reports to understand specific strikes against Kyushu, and to fill in gaps left by the overarching TF Action Reports. Before doing so, researchers made the decision to first gather a list of Bureau Number F4U and F6F aircraft accidents that may have occurred in the TG target areas. The decision to include both aircraft types arose from uncertainty of the provenience, and possibility that the engine and propeller, and the wing piece may be from two separate aircraft. The list, compiled from aircraft accident reports held by the NHHC archives on microfilm, consists of nearly 114 F6F Hellcats and 81 F4U Corsairs that may have possibly gone down in Kyushu (U.S. Navy Bureau of Aeronautics 1945). Many had scarce locational information, some listing loss area as 'Empire' and others listing even less and were therefore included for the sake of a holistic research approach.

The accrued list of aircraft accidents provided a list of possibilities that were then systematically eliminated upon further research of primary documentation. Researchers assessed the Action Reports of the aircraft carriers associated with each TF and cross referenced each aircraft accident by either BuNo when present, or by date. The criteria used are categorized as follows: locational, vicinity to task group, no operations, and jettisoned. The cross referencing of aircraft carrier Action Reports and aircraft accident reports allowed researchers to eliminate most BuNos from the list based on the criteria listed above. Time gaps in the Action Reports did exist, in which case Squadron Histories supplied locational evidence. Douglas E. Campbell's *BuNo! Disposition of World War II USN, USMC and USCG Aircraft Listed by Bureau Number* (2012) supplied some general locational information that helped eliminate some BuNos when no other documentary evidence was available. Seven aircraft, BuNos 72493, 78612, 57723, 82181, 82378, 14458, and one unknown were not eliminated from this list due to lack of locational information. Of those seven aircraft, five were from land based marine squadrons. Land based marine fighters operated on Okinawa after the initial invasion, and it is likely that from Okinawa airfields, sorties and strikes occurred over Kyushu during the subsequent months of war (Tillman 2014). At this time, researchers have not acquired evidence of Kyushu strikes of land-based VMF squadrons; therefore, these five aircraft accidents must remain in the realm of possibilities until proven otherwise.

While researchers were unable to completely cross-reference and eliminate all the BuNos from the list, there were no references of any lost near Saiki. Sorties and strikes are often listed as sweeps in vicinity of specific airfields, and therefore researchers chose a broad area around the area of interest, Saiki. The inclusion of the three closest airfields, Oita, Miyaji, and Usa, allowed for a wider range of potential aircraft accidents. Even with a wider range, no potential accidents materialized. Only with a survey of the Action Reports available did one instance of an F4U lost in Saiki Bay emerge. In the *Intrepid*'s 18 March to 16 April Action Report, in the 'Own Losses and Rescue Operations' table, one F4U-1D is listed as "seen to crash in Saiki Harbor" on 18 March 1945. A further look at the Action Report revealed that the pilot missing in action was Loren Francis Isley. Following is the brief summary of what caused the accident.

> "While participating in 0545 Fighter Sweep against Saeki Airfield, Kyushu Island, plane was going into high speed dive over target and failed to pull out. Plane was seen to crash into waters of Saeki Bay and broke into pieces with no evidence of survivor. Pilot believed to have been hit with AA [Anti-Aircraft] fire. No smoke or damage was observed from plane before crash" (Office of Naval Records and Library 1945n).

While remaining the only positive identification of an aircraft accident in the area, seven BuNos still lie unaccounted for due to lack of documentary evidence. Several more are only discounted due to a secondary source (Campbell 2012). As such, a conclusive identification of the aircraft components is currently unfeasible. The Action Reports of each aircraft carrier, scarce as they are, assisted in this process of elimination.

Conclusions

Of the three broad research questions addressed, researchers were able to answer each to a certain degree with a combination of primary and secondary sources. Unfortunately, gaps in historical documents such as the WWII Action Reports, Squadron Histories, and even Aircraft Parts Manuals prevented a complete representation. The following provides the deductions gathered from each research step.

Aircraft Type Identification

Understanding the artifacts is a preliminary requirement to answer the latter research questions in this case. Reference to Aircraft Parts Manuals and secondary sources fortunately provided enough information to identify the engine as a Pratt & Whitney R-2800. Initial archival research offered enough information to understand that the F6F Hellcat and the F4U Corsair are the only two aircraft to utilize variants of this type of engine around Kyushu by the U.S. Navy in WWII. Further identification is currently unattainable, as the engine components identifying between the two aircraft types are beyond reasonable recognition or missing. As previously mentioned, if a detailed parts catalog exists, future researchers may be able to further identify the engine and propeller. Researchers identified the wing piece as part of an F4U Corsair via visual cues, and comparison of parts manuals of the F6F and F4U. Though it is probable the two artifacts are related to the same aircraft, lack of provenience required researchers to explore both aircraft types.

Timeline of F6F and F4U Usage in Kyushu Area

Extensive action occurred in and around Kyushu during the last year of WWII. Unfortunately, documentary evidence of each individual sweep or strike is spotty. The TF 58 Action Reports provided a general timeline listing Kyushu related attacks, where TF 38 Action Reports did not. The U.S. established attacks on Kyushu in their initial strike of 18 March 1945, providing support to the Okinawa invasion. TF 58 continued various strikes on Kyushu and surrounding islands until its reorganization into TF 38. The newly reorganized TF continued numerous strikes on Kyushu and surrounding areas during the month of June, until the end of the Okinawa campaign. During this time, their focus was directed north at the main island of Honshu in preparation for a final invasion. Strikes against Kyushu continued during this time and until the end of the war, though with less intensity.

Losses in the Vicinity of Saiki Bay

The locational information provided within aircraft accident reports in this area are generally defined as simply 'Empire,' if provided at all. An accumulation of pertinent accident reports provided a stage to eliminate BuNos via the locational information, cross-referenced by Action Reports and other appropriate documents. The initial criteria for accumulating this list were locational or simply unknown. The listed BuNos are only those that did not provide enough information to eliminate immediately. Subsequently, the considerable list of nearly 200 aircraft slowly shrank as Action Reports provided the necessary information for elimination.

As mentioned, a survey of aircraft carrier Action Reports available revealed one reference to an aircraft lost in Saiki Bay on March 18, from the USS *Intrepid*. Currently, this report appears to reveal a potential identity of the aircraft components. However, the seven accident reports that were not eliminated from the list of accident reports leaves the author with doubt. Unfortunately, the reference to this accident was not discovered within the aircraft accident reports. There are potentially other documents that have not survived the archiving process, and thus there may be other aircraft that could have crashed into Saiki Bay. Further archival research is needed to unquestionably identify the aircraft from which the components originate.

The aircraft artifacts still require several years of conservation efforts. Once in a suitable state of preservation, these objects will serve as powerful tools to tell the story of the men and women who served their country in times of strife. Seeing the remnants of a WWII aircraft wrecking event often evokes an emotional connection to those who lost their lives during this time. While the provenience of these artifacts is questionable, they still retain emotional and educative value.

Acknowledgements

I would like to thank the NHHC's Underwater Archaeology Branch for the internship opportunity. The time spent in Washington D.C. with their office was rewarding and educational. This study required numerous weeks at various archival repositories and I would like to acknowledge the archivists of the NHHC, Library of Congress, and National Archives. David Schwartz of the National Air and Space Museum gave considerable assistance while comparing the aircraft manuals to the artifacts. Finally, the author would like to thank Michael Boitnott of the National Museum of Naval Aviation for his time and advice on aircraft construction during this study.

References

Astor, Gerald
1995 *Operation Iceberg: The Invasion and Conquest of Okinawa in World War II*. Penguin, New York.

Campbell, Douglas E.
2012 *BuNos! Disposition of World War II USN, USMC, and USCG Aircraft Listed by Bureau Number*. Syneca Research Group.

Chief of Bureau of Aeronautics
1943 *Structural Repair Instructions for Navy F4U-1, F3A-1, and FG-1*. Chief of the Bureau of Aeronautics. Steven Udvar-Hazy National Air and Space Museum Archives.

1944 *Parts Catalog for Aircraft Engines Models: R-2900-8, -8w, -10, -10w, and -65*. Chief of the Bureau of Aeronautics. Steven Udvar-Hazy National Air and Space Museum Archives.

1945 *Erection and Maintenance Instructions: Model F4U-1, FG-1, F3A-1 Airplanes*. Steven Udvar-Hazy National Air and Space Museum Archives.

1946 *Parts Catalog for Hydromatic Propellers (Hamilton Standard)*. Chief of the Bureau of Aeronautics. Steven Udvar-Hazy National Air and Space Museum Archives.

1947 *Erection and Maintenance Instruction for Navy Model: F6F-3, F6F-3N, F6F-5, F6F-5N Airplanes*. Steven Udvar-Hazy National Air and Space Museum Archives.

Naval History and Heritage Command
2016 *Remains of a WWII Corsair Arrive at NHHC*. <http://www.navy.mil/submit/display.asp?story_id=93761>.

Office of Naval Records and Library
1945a *Action Reports. Third Fleet*. Record Group 38. National Archives Building, College Park, Maryland.

1945b *Action Reports. Fifth Fleet*. Record Group 38. National Archives Building, College Park, Maryland.

1945c *Action Reports. USS Bataan*. Record Group 38. National Archives Building, College Park, Maryland.

1945d *Action Reports. USS Belleau Wood*. Record Group 38. National Archives Building, College Park, Maryland.

1945e *Action Reports. USS Bennington*. Record Group 38. National Archives Building, College Park, Maryland.

1945f *Action Reports. USS Bon Homme Richard*. Record Group 38. National Archives Building, College Park, Maryland.

1945g *Action Reports. USS Bunkerhill*. Record Group 38. National Archives Building, College Park, Maryland.

1945h *Action Reports. USS Cabot*. Record Group 38. National Archives Building, College Park, Maryland.

1945i *Action Reports. USS Enterprise*. Record Group 38. National Archives Building, College Park, Maryland.

1945j *Action Reports. USS Essex*. Record Group 38. National Archives Building, College Park, Maryland.

1945k *Action Reports. USS Hancock*. Record Group 38. National Archives Building, College Park, Maryland.

1945l *Action Reports. USS Hornet*. Record Group 38. National Archives Building, College Park, Maryland.

1945m *Action Reports. USS Independence*. Record Group 38. National Archives Building, College Park, Maryland.

1945n *Action Reports. USS Intrepid*. Record Group 38. National Archives Building, College Park, Maryland.

1945o *Action Reports. USS Monterey*. Record Group 38. National Archives Building, College Park, Maryland.

1945p   *Action Reports. USS Randolph.* Record Group 38. National Archives Building, College Park, Maryland.

1945q   *Action Reports. USS San Jacinto.* Record Group 38. National Archives Building, College Park, Maryland.

1945r   *Action Reports. USS Shangri-La.* Record Group 38. National Archives Building, College Park, Maryland.

1945s   *Action Reports. Task Force 38.* Record Group 38. National Archives Building, College Park, Maryland.

1945t   *Action Reports. Task Force 58.* Record Group 38. National Archives Building, College Park, Maryland.

1945u   *Action Reports. USS Ticonderoga.* Record Group 38. National Archives Building, College Park, Maryland.

1945v   *Action Reports. USS Wasp.* Record Group 38. National Archives Building, College Park, Maryland.

1945w   *Action Reports. USS Yorktown.* Record Group 38. National Archives Building, College Park, Maryland.

Sherman, Frederick C.
1950   *Combat Command.* Dutton.

Tillman, Barrett
1979   *Corsair: The F4U in World War II and Korea.* Naval Institute Press.

2014   *US Marine Corps Fighter Squadrons of World War II.* Osprey Publishing.

U.S. Navy Bureau of Aeronautics
1945   *F4U, FG, and F6F Aircraft Accident Reports.* Microfilm. NHHC Archives. Washington D.C.

White, Graham
1995   *Allied Aircraft Piston Engines of World War II.* Society of Automotive Engineers.

2001   *R-2800: Pratt & Whitney's dependable masterpiece.* Society of Automotive Engineers.

• • • • • • • • • • • • • • • •

Hunter W. Whitehead
The Division of Anthropology and Archaeology
University of West Florida
11000 University Parkway
Pensacola, FL 32514
(850) 368-2591
h.w.whitehead3@gmail.com

An Account of Stone Anchors: A Study of Northern Shoreline of the Persian Gulf

Sorna Khakzad, Ali Moosaie

This paper presents an inventory of the historical stone anchors observed along the northern shoreline of the Persian Gulf. This collection was put together through site observation, documentation, and archival study. Findings were observed and recorded, in part, during ongoing construction and development in the case study areas. The documentation includes recording the locations of the objects by Global Positioning System (GPS), their weights, sizes, photos and drawings that resulted in classification of these anchors. The results of this research can lead us to more in-depth studies about seafaring and maritime history in the Persian Gulf.

Introduction

Three major bodies of water are adjacent to Iran. There are more than 989 km of shoreline along the Persian Gulf, 784 km along the Oman Sea, and more than 800 km along the Caspian Sea (Dibajnia et al. 2012:1; IHO 1953:20-21). Present-day Iran was historically part of the larger empire of Persia (550 BC-AD 1925). According to historical sources and studies, Persian seafaring dates back at least to the Sassanid era (AD 224-651) (Hourani 1950:36-46; Le Strange 1966:257-69, 295-8; Agius 2008:75; Whitehouse and Williamson 1973:29-49). Despite an extensive Persian maritime history, only a few attempts to write exclusively about Persian naval history, such as Hasan (A History of Persian Navigation 1928) and Raeen (*Daryanavardiye Iranian:* Iranian Navigation 1971) have been published. Some background studies about Persian maritime history can be found in Greek literature (Herodotus 1920; Diodorus Siculus 1946), travelers' accounts (Freeman-Grenville 1982:63-70; Ferrand 1922:7, 26, 53-58) and artworks. This paper will present one aspect of Iranian maritime history by examining an inventory of stone anchors that were observed and recorded in a number of historic ports and villages along the shoreline of Bushehr. Several studies on anchor typology from the Persian Gulf have been published (Vosmer 1999; Bowen 1957), but no study has exclusively focused on stone anchors found in Iran and the northern shorelines of the Persian Gulf.

Throughout the maritime history of the Persian Gulf, stone anchors were in regular use. The Persian glossary, *Miftah-ul fuzala*, compiled during the second half of the 15th century at Mandu (Malwa), defines langar (anchor) as the 'stone of a kishti' (boat) (Hourani 1951; Tripati et al. 2005:131-137; Qaisar and Verma 2002:20). Among the sporadic documentation of Iranian stone anchors, three stone anchors were reported by Whitehouse (1970:141), found at terrestrial archaeological sites in Siraf; two were recorded in the 2012 investigations in Siraf (Khakzad et al. 2014); and one single-holed, round-shape anchor was reported in the port of Ganaveh, about 100 km northwest of Busher (Tofighian 2014). For classification purpose, the present work relies on studies from other parts of the world, such as India and the southern shorelines of the Persian Gulf.

Stone Anchors

Stone anchors are made of a stone shank in a variety of shapes and are known from different parts of the world (Tripati et al. 1998; 2005; Frost et al. 1993). These anchors have varying numbers and shapes of holes; some anchors have flukes and some do not. A stone anchor may be nothing more than a heavy stone with a hole for its line, which relies on weight alone. Stone anchors have been documented illustrating a wide range of shapes and sizes of stone with several piercings for wooden or iron arms that dig into the seafloor, and one hole for the cable (Frost et al. 1993:449; Carter 2005:140; Lorimer 1915:2229; Potts 1998:148). Studying stone anchors is important for understanding types of ancient ships, their size, their function, and their location of origin, as well as for hypothesizing the geographical passage and anchorage of ships in the history of navigation (Frost 1963:2).

Stone Anchors from Persian Gulf Countries

Studies conducted on the southern side of the Persian Gulf in Qatar, Oman and United Arab Emirates (UAE) recorded a number of stone anchors including different types of Indo-Arabian, composite stone anchors and *al sinn* anchors (e.g. Qalhat anchor) (Vosmer 1999:250-252). Indo-Arabian stone anchors are plinth type (a long frustum-shaped stone) with a round hole at the smaller end and two perpendicularly opposed rectangular holes at the larger end. Indo-Arabian stone anchors are also recorded in the western Indian Ocean and Arabian Sea (Vosmer 1999:251). Composite stone anchors are triangular, often made of a flat thin block, with a circular upper hole at the apex and two holes at the lower side (Tripati and Caesar 2015). *al sinn* is a rectangular-shaped anchor, mostly recorded with one hole on the flat face and another on the side, described since the early 16th century (Badger 1863:59-60; Pilcher et al. 2003:38; Agius 2008:144-146; de Ruyter 2014:126-127). According to previous studies, *al sinn* anchors indicate the passage or wreck of an Arab or Persian fishing or pearling vessel in the Gulf (de Ruyter 2014:128; Agius 2012:182). LeBaron Bowen stated that *al sinn* stone anchors located on the Iranian littoral possibly are indigenous to that coast (Bowen 1957:293). This study, also, introduces evidence that confirms this type of anchor was locally made in Iran.

Methodology

For the current study, data were collected through the documentation of coastal cultural heritage and archaeological sites, and visiting construction sites, mainly reported by local people. The artifact assemblage consists of surface finds, and no archaeological excavation occurred. Similar to some surviving examples of *al sinn* anchors, such as those in museums in the UAE (Sharjah Maritime Museum and Dubai), the Iranian *al sinn* anchors were found on land along with archaeological remains, or at local residences and shipyards (Blau 1995:120-124; Carter 2005:168). In addition, several stone shanks and anchors were identified underwater. A few stone anchors were discovered as a result of digging for foundations of new buildings and road construction. These artifacts have mainly been found in locations and sites that are threatened by, or have already undergone, urban and industrial development. Some data were collected through communicating with local people and fishermen, who have stone anchors in their possession from past generations.

As learned from other studies, the primary recording methodology consists of drawing, photographing, documenting size and weight measurements, describing form and materials, and explaining holes and their directions. Frost mentions that size and weight are the two most important measurements to record because these two measurements usually indicate the size of the ship that carried the anchor (Frost 1997:122). The finder or reporter of the artifacts also recorded the GPS location of the findings. Artifacts in danger of destruction or loss were transported to museums, documented, and archived in the museums. Anchors in possession of individuals were photographed, weighed, and the location of their finding, if known by the owner, was recorded. The process of documentation provided a training opportunity for local people. Through talking to local people and local non-governmental organizations (NGOs) about the importance of archaeological sites and, in this case, stone anchors, they are now more aware of the cultural importance of these artifacts, and they are more likely to share their findings and the location of other discoveries with archaeologists. In total, more than 300 stone anchors were recorded. Some of them are smaller in shape and lighter in weight, which were categorized as stone fishing weights. We did not have enough information and tools to date the stone anchors. The following sections present the analysis of these stone anchors and stone weights.

Study Areas and Findings

The study area covers the shoreline of Bushehr Province, where several important historical ports and traditional fishing villages are located. The research sites were selected from among important archaeological and historical sites in danger of destruction or loss of archaeological artifacts.

Rishahr

Rishahr, now located within the city of Bushehr, was one of the major ports in the Persian Gulf. Rishahr, historically known as Rev Ardeshir, was an Elamite city and an important port during the reign of King Ardeshir (180–242 AD) (Massoudi 2013:146; Daryaee 2008; Kazeruni 2015:60). Currently, remains of Rishahr are located in and around a large extended cliff, which varies in height along the shoreline and in some locations reaches 10 m (33 ft). The site includes remnants of a collapsed well and human remains, in addition to several types of carved stones and stone blocks within different layers of the cliff and on the shoreline. Previous archaeological studies (Whitehouse and Williamson 1973; Ataie 2005) recorded remains of an ancient pier or wave break, extending from the shoreline to the sea. Among the remains, several stone shanks and anchor

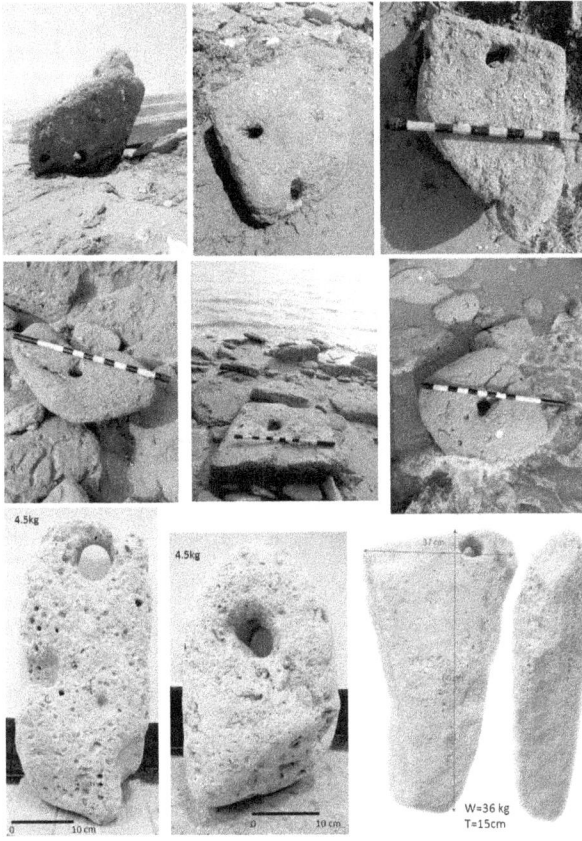

FIGURE 1: Several stone artifacts, classified as stone anchors and potential anchors, were observed in Rishahr, Iran. The artifacts were located close to the potential ancient pier/wavebreak and on the beach along the bay.

types were documented. Some peculiar stone objects, whose function has yet to be identified, also were noted (Figure 1).

Moving Southeast from Rishahr towards Siraf, local people reported a few more anchors. While composite three-holed anchors are very common in the Mediterranean, and examples have been found on the Arabian side of the Persian Gulf (Raban 2000:260; Frost et al 1993:452), the only three-holed composite anchor observed, so far, within our case study area came from the archaeological site of Bardu in Bardestan (See figure 4, last row).

Siraf

Siraf is a coastal town, well-known historically by national and international archaeologists. Extensive terrestrial archaeological excavations and some underwater cultural heritage studies have been conducted near this town (Whitehouse 1968, 1969, 1970, 1971, 1972, Masoumi 2004; Khakzad et al. 2014). Through these studies, three Indo-Arabian anchors were reported by Whitehouse (1970:14-15), and three single-holed anchors were observed (two documented) during 2012 studies (Khakzad et al. 2014). Among those recorded during the 2012 project, one was possibly a single-holed ring-stone, observed underwater, which was badly eroded; one was a pear-shaped, single-holed anchor, recorded underwater and left in situ; and the last one was half of a broken single-holed, pear-shaped anchor found among debris on the beach. In addition, several millstones were observed along the shoreline that could have been used as mooring buoys.

Nayband

Nayband is located about 60 km southeast of Siraf. Here, the remains of a wave break and historic ruins can be seen. Archaeologists have identified some of the buildings among the ruins along the coast as trade, storage, and customs buildings (Esmaili Jelodar & Ebrahimi, 2012). Nyaband was mentioned in historical records, and travelers and historians such as Yaqout (1959), Al Muqaddasi (1906), and Ibn Hawqal (1965) described this city as a port and a good anchorage area for ships around the 9th to 11th centuries. Terrestrial archaeological studies on this site have documented its archaeological and maritime historical significance (Esmaili Jelodar and Ebrahimi 2012). More than 200 stone anchors and stone weights have been located at this site (Figure 2). Most of these artifacts were observed in terrestrial sites among the rubble. Only one anchor was recorded in the tidal area. More extensive underwater excavations and studies need to be conducted on this site yet. Several stone artifacts that seem to represent incomplete stone anchors were also observed in this site.

Bostano

Residents of a village in Hormozgan Province, neighboring Boushehr Province, have been engaged in fishing for many generations. Although, the present buildings are not historical, there are records of archaeological remains beneath and around the village, and the area has been identified as historically important by international scholars (Stein 1937:199). Although the study areas were mainly in Bushehr Province, some local people from Bostano reported finding stone anchors. These artifacts were found by local people digging wells or foundations for new buildings. These anchors are larger in size (about 60-75 cm (24-30 in) high) in comparison with the ones found in Nayband and Siraf (maximum 50 cm (20 in)), and are similar to the type called al-sinn (Figure 3). Among them, is one anchor

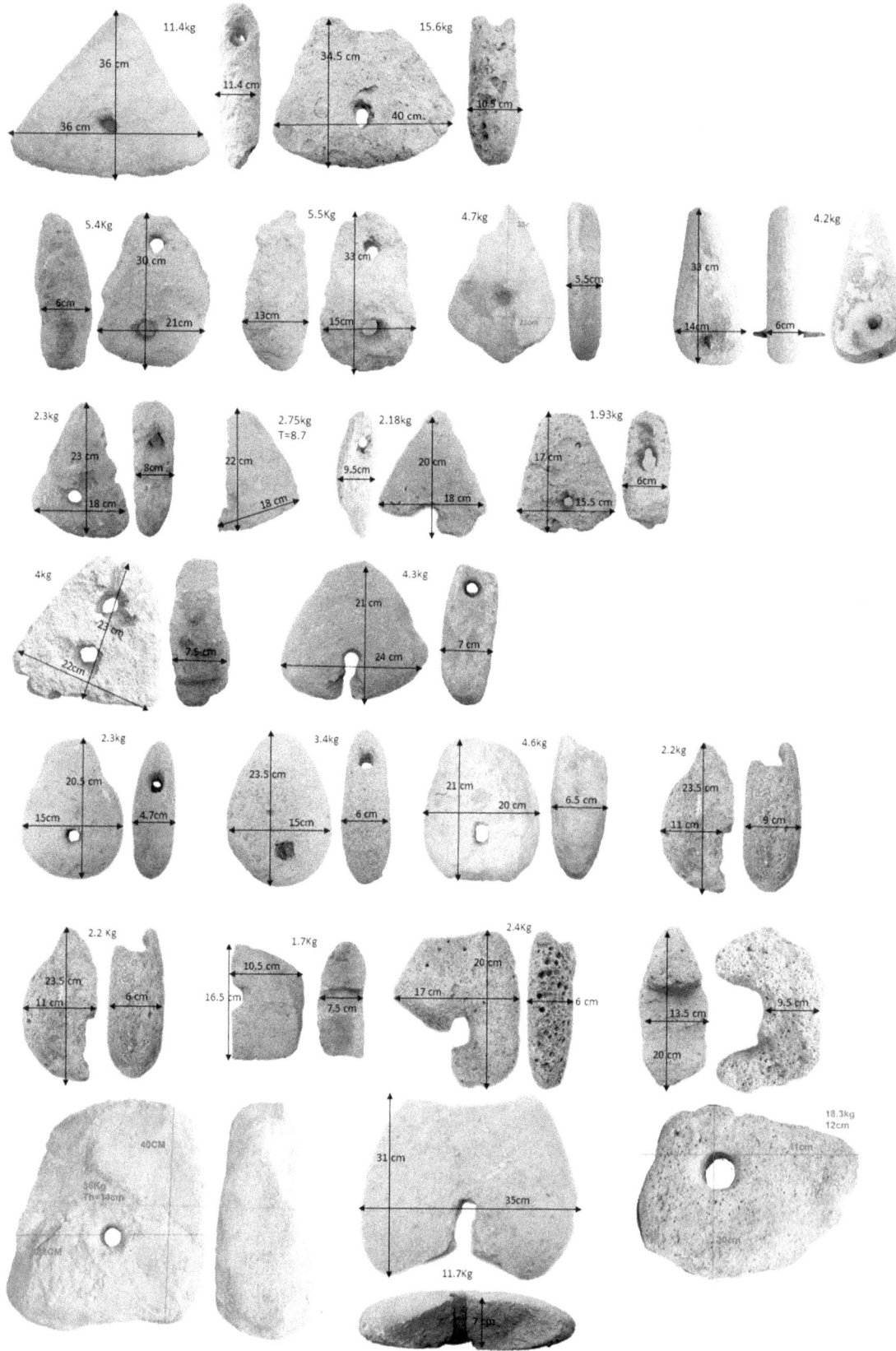

FIGURE 2: Examples of stone anchors documented at the Nayband Site. They include a variety sizes and shapes. Some of them are badly eroded, and some are in better shape. One was recorded with its iron fluke still inside its hole.

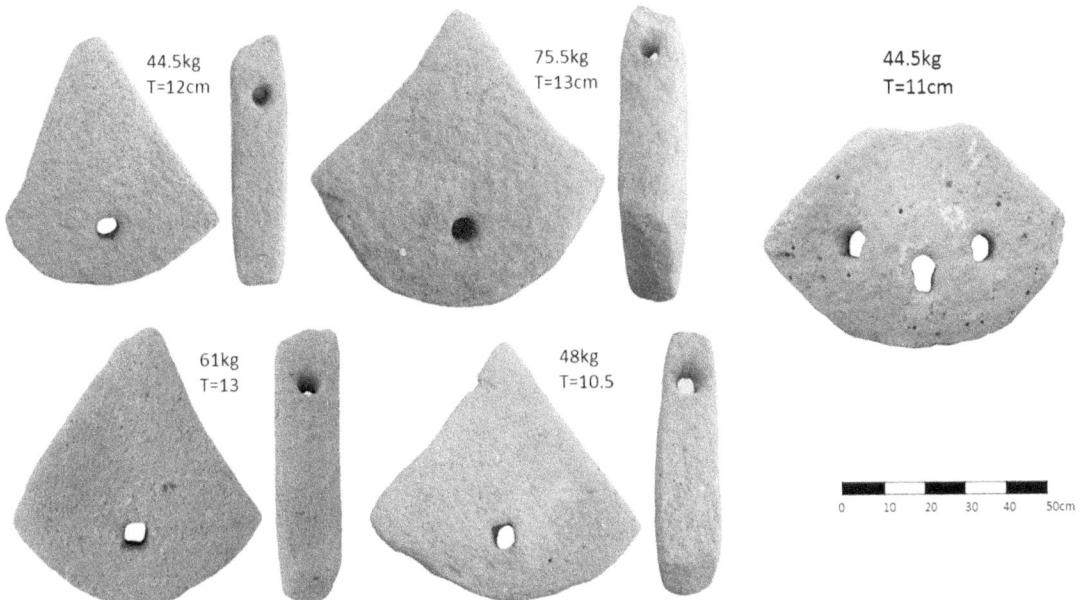

FIGURE 3: Anchors documented in Bostano are similar to the type called al-sinn. Four of this type are reported that are in good shape, while one is broken (right).

which is slightly different from others; this anchor is the only one that has been recorded with three holes on the surface. The upper part of the anchor is broken, so it is not possible to determine anything about its side hole (Figure 4, first row). It was donated to the Bushehr Museum by a local person who found it while digging a well on his property at a depth of about one meter.

Through this study, the authors documented three anchors in Rishahr, 15 weights in Hezar Mardan, 32 weights and anchors in Bibi-Khatoon, more than 200 in Nayband (and still counting), five anchors in Siraf, and six reported in Bostano by local people. We observed 19 weights in Javado'l Aemeh, 12 in Beloghreh, and 17 in Zyarat. The stone anchors and weights in Bushehr Province, which were in danger of loss and destruction, in addition to those donated by local people, were transferred to the Museum of Maritime Trade in Bushehr.

Typology and Classification

Frost (1997) identified several different criteria for stone anchor classification, which were utilized by the authors for this study. Characteristics of the artifacts that could be accurately and precisely recorded, such as weight, size and number of holes, were documented. The results indicate that there are several types and forms of stone anchors, with different weights, and varying numbers and shapes of the holes. One additional consideration is the type or materials used in the manufacture of stone anchors, which was included in this study. The type of stone used in the construction of anchors can provide further information on the stone's possible origin. Of the stone anchors examined, local geologists identified the materials used as sandstone, limestone or corals; all of which exist locally in the mountains as well as along the rocky coastline. However, not all types of anchor stone were specifically identified. The results of our classification are presented in the following seven major groups (Figure 4).

Large Al-sinn Type

The first group of similar stone anchors is the large al-sinn type reported by local people in Bostano. Heights range from 50 cm to 70 cm, and weights between 45 to 75 kg. They all have one hole on the surface, and one hole on the side (the form of the side holes was not recorded, just the location is noted). Among these anchors, one is exceptional with three holes on the surface. We called this one "Persian-Bostano Type." One large *al sinn* type from Nayband is lighter in weight in comparison with the ones from Bostano. Therefore, due to its shape and weight, it is classified under the category small al-sinn type.

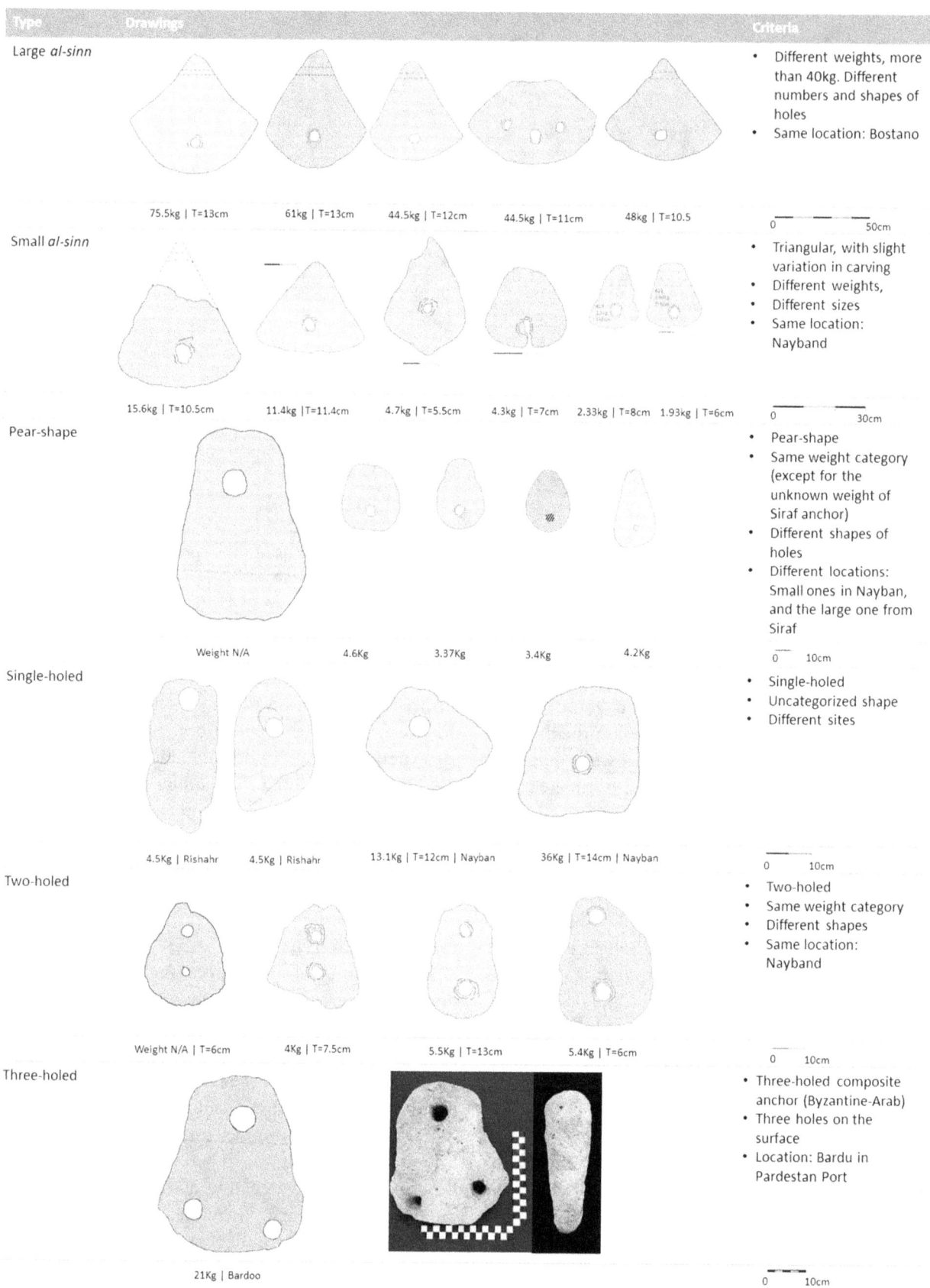

FIGURE 4: Classification of stone anchors based on different criteria of weight, size, shape, number of holes, and location of finding.

Small Al-sinn Type

These anchors vary in their sizes (height varies between ~15 cm to ~40 cm), weights (varies between 2 kg to ~18 kg), thickness (varies between 5.5 and 11.4 cm), and carving style (flat, pointed, or curved bottom). Some of these anchors are badly damaged, broken or eroded, therefore the exact location of the side hole and its form is unclear. Among this type, one was found uncompleted. These types were recorded in Nayband.

Pear-Shaped Type

A number of stone anchors with a pear shape, with one hole on the side and one hole on the surface, or only one hole on the surface, were recorded from Nayband and Siraf. However, their forms vary to some extent, and the shapes of their surface holes are different as well. Their heights vary between 20 cm to 50 cm, and they weigh between 2.5 kg to 5 kg. The Siraf anchor is larger in comparison with the ones from Nayband. The ones from Nayband can be considered big weights rather than anchors.

Single-Holed Type

Several single-holed anchors, in a variety of shapes, were recorded from Nayband and Rishahr. We put them in the single-holed group with uncategorized shape. Their sizes, weights, and thicknesses vary.

Two-Holed Type

Four two-hole anchors, different in form, were recorded in Nayband. The two holes are on their surface. Their heights are between 20 cm to ~30 cm, and weights between 4 kg to 5.5 kg. However, they are eroded and their original weight and shapes are not completely identifiable. Their thickness varies between 6 cm to 13 cm as well.

Three-Holed type

Three-holed composite anchors, also known as Byzantine-Arab, are the triangular- or trapezoidal-shaped stone anchors with three holes on the surface, used for sandy and rocky seabed (Frost 1963). Only one of this type was recorded during our investigations, found by local people, in the archaeological site of Bardu in Bardestan Port, about 40 km northwest of Siraf. It weighs about 21 kg.

Stone Weights

The smaller stones were classified as weights. However, we found varieties of weights from a simple rock with evidence of a rope wrapped around it, to more sophisticated and carved stones, either flat or bulky, and with or without a hole in the middle. They were categorized based on the existence of holes, and the side that a rope was tied around. These stone weights were recorded in many sites such as Nayband, Rishahr, Bostano, and all the fishing villages. An in depth study of fishing techniques and vessels can reveal more clear use of these weights for fishing. In addition, among our findings are at least three stone anchors identified as unfinished (incomplete). They appear to be from al-sinn type and pear-shaped types. These unfinished artifacts are evidence these types of anchors were made locally in these locations.

Discussion and Conclusion

Through the present study, more than 300 stone anchors and weights were documented. We classified these findings based on their shapes, weights, the number of holes, and their location of recovery. The stone types and materials were not applied for this classification, since we did not have the possibility to identify all the stone types. Classification was not a simple task, because some types are exceptional, and some types are similar in some ways and not in other ways. Our observation and analysis conclude as follows:

Anchors types and weights from certain towns and ports appear to be very specific to those areas, and we have not observed many similar types in other ports, villages, or towns in our study areas. This may indicate that the production or use of some of these anchors was localized for limited local fishing, pearl hunting, or small-scale trade. For instance, we can hypothesize that the concentration of a specific type of stone weight in villages such as Bibi-Khatun or Hezar-Mardan might indicate different uses for stone weights. The al sinn type, from Bostano, might be indicative of the concentration of pearl hunting in this area. However, more archaeological evidence is needed to prove any of these hypotheses.

Unfinished anchors of different types, possibly al sinn and pear-shaped, that were documented can be an indication that these types of anchors were made in those locations. In addition, the types of stone and rock used for anchor and weight production are similar to the local stone from surrounding mountains, such as limestone and granite. Therefore, it can be strongly concluded that some of the stone anchors in the collection are locally sourced. This is an important argument when it comes to the production of al sinn anchors, and indicates the

Iranian side of the Persian Gulf was engaged in wider maritime activities and seafaring trading with other countries.

Concentration of many stone anchors and weights in Nayband can shed more light on the importance of this port. Its closeness to Siraf is peculiar in the sense that it raises questions about the function of Siraf as a major port. Nayband has a more protected bay, and a better anchorage area. A hypothesis can be raised regarding whether Nayband and Siraf were working together, and whether Nayband was used as an anchorage area instead of Siraf for trade and sheltering ships. This is a question that needs further study.

In addition to scientific findings, this study helped raise awareness among local people about the historical importance of these anchors and weights. This in return resulted in additional site observation by local people and more reports of finding stone anchors and weights. Therefore, the documentation of weights and anchors has become an ongoing process. In addition, raising awareness helped encourage local NGOs and cultural heritage offices to organize exhibitions and set up local museum exhibits to show these artifacts.

Lastly, the inventory this study conducted provides opportunity for more research on stone anchors and stone artifacts observed in different historical ports and archaeological sites. This inventory can be used to start a database for future comparative analysis with such artifacts from other locations in the world. Moreover, our findings, from sites such as Rishahr and Nayband, raised new questions about different artifacts, their functions, and the location of important ports and anchorage areas.

Future work should include preservation of the finds and presentation of the results to researchers and the public. More underwater studies, close to the historical ports, can reveal more stone anchors and additional cultural heritage. These studies should be incorporated into the larger body of maritime history studies in Iran. Comparison studies of the relation between anchor/weight typology and their locations can help to understand seafaring and maritime trade among different ports inside and outside the Persian Gulf.

Acknowledgements

The authors would like to express their gratitude to Drs. Abdol Karim Mashayekhi, Director of Museum of Maritime Trade in Bushehr; Iraj Nabipour, Director of Persian Gulf Biotechnology Research Center (Zist Fanavari); Mr. Mohammad Kangani, Director of Siraf Pars Museum, for their scientific and logistic support; local people, who provided information about the archaeological sites and the location of artifacts, and for donating their artifacts to the museum; Mrs. Soheila Dejam Shahabi for her administrative support. Finally, many thanks to Florida Public Archaeology Network for providing financial support to present this paper at Society for Historical Archaeology's Conference on Historical and Underwater Archaeology.

References

AGIUS, DIONISIUS
2002 Qalhat: A port of embarkation for India. In *Studies in Arabic and Islam*, S. Leder, editor, pp. 32-35. Peeters Publishing, Leuven.

AGIUS, DIONISIUS
2008 *Classic ships of Islam from Mesopotamia to the Indian Ocean*. Leiden. Boston.

AGIUS, DIONISIUS
2012 *Seafaring in the Arabian Gulf and Oman: People of the Dhow (1st ed.)*. Taylor and Francis, Hoboken.

AL-MUQADDASI
1906 *Ahsan al-Taqasim fo Ma'rifat al-Aqlam*. M. J., de Goeje, translator and editor, Bibliotheca Geographorum Arabicorum, Leiden.

ATAIE, MOHAMMAD
2005 Archaeological reports in Rishahr shoreline, Bushehr: Development of local kings' territory. *Archaeological Reports*, No. 1, Iran.

BADGER, GEORGE PERCY (EDITOR)
1863 *The travels of Ludovico Di Varthema in Egypt, Syria, Arabia Deserta and Arabia Felix, in Persia, India, and Ethiopia, AD. 1503 to 1508*, J. W. Jones, translator. The Hakluyt Society of London.

BLAU, SOREN
1995 Observing the present—reflecting the past: attitude towards archaeology in the United Arab Emirates. In *Arabian Archaeology and Epigraphy* 6:116-128, John Wiley & Sons.

BOWEN, LEBARON R., JR.
1957 Arab Anchors. *The Mariner's Mirror* 43(4): 288-293, DOI: 10.1080/00253359.1957.10658361

CARTER, ROBERT
2005 The History and Prehistory of Pearling in the Persian Gulf. *Journal of the Economic and Social History of The Orient* 48(2): 139-209.

DARYAEE, TOURAJ
2008 *The rise and fall of an Empire*, 1st edition. I B Tauris & Co Ltd., London.

DE RUYTER, MICHAEL.
2014   Al Sinn: Stone anchor of the Persian Gulf pearl fishery. *Bulletin of the Australasian Institute for Maritime Archaeology* 38: 125-129

DIBAJNIA, MOHAMMAD, MOHSEN SOLTANPOUR, FREYDON VAFAI, AND AMIR JAZAYERI
2012   A Shoreline Management Plan for Iranian coastlines. In *Ocean & Coastal Management* 63: 1-15.

DIODORUS SICULUS
1946   *Library of History,* XI, 3, F. W. Walton, translator. Loeb Classical Library. 10.1016/j.ocecoaman.2012.2.12

ESMAILI JELODAR, EBRAHIM. AND N. EBRAHIMI
2012   Re-identification of New Ports in the Gulf of Nayband based on Archaeological Evidences and Documents. *Gamaneh* 3.

FERRAND, GABRIEL (TRANSLATOR)
1922   *Voyage du marchand arab Sulayman en Inde et en Chine. Redige en 851, suivi remar ques par Abu Zayad Hasan* (c.916). Paris

FREEMAN-GRENVILLE, G. S. P. (EDITOR)
1982   *Some Thoughts on Buzurg Ibn Shahryar al-Ramhourmuzi, The Book of the Wonders of India,* Paideuma: Mitteilungen zur Kulturkunde 28: 63–70.

FROST, HONOR
1963   From Rope to Chain on the Development of Anchors in the Mediterranean, *The Mariner's Mirror* 49(1): 1-20. DOI: 10.1080/00253359.1963.10657711

1997   Stone Anchors: The need for methodological recording. *Indian Journal of History of Science,* 32 (2), pp. 121-126.

FROST, HONOR, H. J. K. JENKINS, DAVID HEPPER, BRIAN S. KIRBY, AND J. PACITTI
1993   NOTES. *The Mariner's Mirror,* 79:4, pp. 449-467. DOI: 10.1080/00253359.1993.10656474

HASSAN, HADI
1928   *A History of Persian Navigation.* Routledge, London

HERODOTUS
1920   *Volume VII,* 89, Alfred Denis Godley, translator, Harvard University Press.

HOURANI, GEORGES. F.
1950   *Arab Seafaring.* Princeton: Princeton University Press

HOURANI, GEORGE. F.
1951   *Arab Seafaring in the Indian Ocean in Ancient and Early Medieval Times.* Princeton University Press, Princeton.

IBN HAWQAL,
1965   *Kitab Surat al-Ard.* Johannes Hendrik Kramers, translator and editor. Bibliotheca Geographorum Arabicorum, Leiden

(IHO) INTERNATIONAL HYDROGRAPHIC ORGANIZATION
1953   *Limits of Oceans and Seas.* Special Publication No. 23, 3rd edition. <https://epic.awi.de/id/eprint/29772/1/IHO1953a.pdf>. Accessed 7 February 2010.

KAZERUNI, MOHAMMAD
2015   *Historical Geography of the Ports and Islands of the Persian Gulf (Original book in Persian language).* Malek National Museum and Library, Iran

KHAKZAD, SORNA, ATENA TRAKADAS, MATTHEW HARPSTER, AND NICOLE WITTIG
2014   Maritime Aspects of Medieval Siraf, Iran: A pilot project for the investigation of coastal and underwater archaeological remains. *International Journal of Nautical Archaeology,* 44(2): 258-276. DOI:10.1111/1095-9270.12085

LE STRANGE, GUY
1966   *The Lands of Eastern Caliphate.* Cambridge University Press, London.

LORIMER, JOHN. G.
1915   *Gazetteer of the Persian Gulf, Oman and Central Arabia. Volume 1: Historical Calcutta.* Irish Academic Press, Ireland.

MASOUMI, G.
2004   Siraf (Taheri Port). *Anjoman Asar va Mafakher Farhangi.* University Press, Tehran (Source in Persian Language).

MASSOUDI, CYRUS
2013   *Land of the Turquoise Mountains: Journeys Across Iran,* 1st edition. I. B. Tauris, London.

PILCHER, N., PHILLIPS, R. C., ASPINAL, S., AL-MADANY, I., KING, H., HELLYER, P., BEECH, M., GILLESPIE, C., WOOD, S., SCHWARZE, H., AL DOSARY, M., AL FARRAJ, I., KHALIFA, A. AND BOER, B.
2003   Hawar Islands Protected Area (Kingdom of Bahrain) Management Plan. UNESCO, Doha.

POTTS, DANIEL. T.
1998   Seas of Change. In *Waves of Time: The Maritime History of the United Arab Emirates.* Peter Hellyer, editor, pp. 47-67. Trident Press, London

QAISAR, A. JAN, AND SOM PRAKASH VERMA (EDITORS)
2002   Chapter 1: The *Miftah-ul Fuzala*: A study of an illustrated Persian Lexicon. In *Art and Culture: Painting and Perspective, Vol. 2,* p. 20.

RABAN, AVNER
2000   Three-hole Composite Stone Anchors from a Medieval Context at Caesarea Maritima, Israel. *The International Journal of Nautical Archaeology* 29(2): 260-272.

RAEEN, ESMAEL.
1971   *Daryanavardie Iranian*, Sekeh, Tehran (Source in Persian language).

STEIN, AUREL
1937   *Archaeological Reconnaissance in North Western India and South Eastern Iran*. MacMillian and Company, London.

TOFIGHIAN, HOSSEIN.
2014   *Pajoohesh haye bastanshenasie Iran* 6: 4. (Source in Persian language)

TRIPATI, SILA AND CAESAR BITA
2015   Stone anchors from Mombasa, Kenya: Evidence of maritime contacts with Indian Ocean countries. *Journal of the Australasian Institute for Maritime Archaeology* 39: 84-91

TRIPATI, SILA, A. MANIKFAN AND M. MOHAMED
2005   An Indo-Arabian Type of Stone Anchor from Kannur, Kerala, West Coast of India. International *Journal of Nautical Archaeology* 34(1): 131-137.

TRIPATI, SILA, A. S. GAUR, SUNDARESH, AND S. N. BANDODKER
1998   Historical Period Stone Anchors from Vijaydurg on the West Coast of India. *Bulletin of the Australian Institute for Maritime Archaeology* 22: 1-8.

VOSMER, THOMAS
1999   Indo-Arabian Stone Anchors in the Western Indian Ocean and Arabian Sea. *Arabian Archaeology and Epigraphy* 10(2): 248-263.

WHITEHOUSE, DAVID
1968   Excavations at Siraf: First Interim Report. *Iran* 6: 1-22.

1969   Excavations at Siraf: Second Interim Report. *Iran* 7: 39-62.

1970   Excavation at Siraf: Third Interim Report. *Iran* 8: 1-18.

1971   Excavations at Siraf: Fourth Interim Report. *Iran* 9: 1-17.

1972   Excavations at Siraf: Fifth Interim Report. *Iran* 10: 63-87.

WHITEHOUSE, DAVID AND ANDREW WILLIAMSON
1973   Sassanian Maritime Trade. *Iran* 11: 29-49.

YAQOUT
1959   The Introductory Chapters of *Mu'jam al Buldan*. Leiden.

• • • • • • • • • • • • • • • •

Sorna Khakzad
207 E Main Street, FPAN Office
Pensacola, Florida 32502
+1 (252) 347 2675
skhakzad@uwf.edu

Ali Moosaie
56 Boostan Alley, Pardis Complex, Jam, Bushehr, Iran
+98 (917) 174 3749
amoosaie82@gmail.com

Survey Says…: Using Archaeological Lenses and Conservation Assessment Tools to Influence Curation

Hannah Fleming, Lesley Haines

Museums often collect objects around broad themes which can lead to the acquisition of artifacts based on varied criteria like time period, culture, technology, condition, aesthetic appeal, and rarity. This is the case for The Mariners' Museum and Park, where "we connect people to the world's waterways." With such an expansive scope – and over 32,000 three-dimensional objects, collected since 1930 - how can one possibly prioritize interpretation, research, and care? This question, combined with the need to address inadequate storage of a portion of the collection, led Museum personnel to develop a survey system that combines archaeological lenses and recording techniques with conservation assessment tools, with the goal of better understanding interpretive criteria (typological and story-based) and the artifacts' conservation needs. With revision, this survey will be applicable to other collections to help re-focus museum prioritization on cultural interpretation and collections care.

Introduction

Prioritization within archaeological collections is necessary because of the sheer volume of material which is recovered and stored. Complete examination and conservation of assemblages can span decades. The Mariners' Museum and Park in Newport News, Virginia, faces a similar problem. The institution has collected since the 1930s and contains over 32,000 objects, along with one of the largest maritime libraries in the Western Hemisphere. Therefore it was not possible, for various reasons, to systematically survey the entirety of the collection. This means that current Museum staff are unable to gauge or utilize the institution's holdings to its full extent.

In spring 2017, Museum personnel were asked to assess the needs of 247 artifacts in long-term exterior storage behind the Museum, as well as 76 artifacts on display around its 550-acre Park. The objects were mainly industrial in size and were left in outdoor storage for a number of years because there was no room inside. The project was initially intended to identify issues with the storage space and to present potential mediation options; however, it also resulted in the development of an assessment system. This holistic approach ranked artifacts based on their conservation needs and their relative significance to the Museum mission. The integration of archaeological lenses and collections care tools was vital in establishing a realistic method of statistically analyzing the collection of artifacts.

Methodology

The artifacts stored outside were a loosely grouped, heterogeneous mix of over-sized anchors, industrial components, and miscellaneous items which had amassed throughout the Museum's 90 years of collecting. Many had lost their labels, over a third were partially buried, and several were from archaeological contexts. Therefore, the Museum made the conscious decision to assess this collection archaeologically, using deposition and typological data, in an effort to provide context for an assemblage that was overlooked for over 50 years.

After initial observations, it was determined that an archaeologist and an archaeological conservator should assess the collection for artifacts' significance and conservation needs, respectively. Staff studied related survey theory and methodology to assist in the development of an assessment system that both fit the unique collection to be surveyed and encompassed the wide range of factors necessary to determine stability and significance.

The surveyors developed a system of two forms, one to assess significance and one to assess condition; each of which scored an artifact based on a specific set of criteria. The two scores were then combined to create the object's overall priority score. While the created forms were initially meant for use on the outdoor collection, surveyors made the forms adaptable for a variety of collections.

During development, the surveyors quickly realized that, to keep significance and condition equal, there needed to be isolation in the forms representing each facet. After form creation, the surveyors worked independently of one another to prevent survey bias in data collection. In order to apply it to the large, diverse, and at-risk outdoor collection, the survey was conducted through steps in the following order: 1) understanding the breadth of the collection to be studied; 2) conducting historical research into the types of artifacts surveyed; 3) completing the historical significance and conservation survey paperwork (independently); 4) artifact specific historical research, and/or extra testing for health and safety issues; 5) compiling the significance and conservation priority data into a single score used to rank overall priority; 6) data processing based on the research questions; 7) interpretation and discussion.

While surveyors worked simultaneously in step three, they did not discuss condition or historical significance with one another. This theoretically limited survey bias as the conservator did not know the historical significance of an artifact, nor did the archaeologist know the conservation needs. Similarly, the format of this survey was intended to examine the collection from the standpoint of a third party, to determine how much information could be gleaned about the objects without institutional knowledge. This intentional isolation also reduced the likelihood of other parties' biases interfering with the dataset. Finally, once the data were compiled into a single and sortable database, the surveyors discussed ways in which to delineate, sort, and interpret the data to answer research questions and complete project aims.

Methodological Limitations

There is no perfect survey method and there were limitations to this data collection process. These limitations do not negate the usefulness of the data, discussion, and recommendations provided, but it is important to note them.

Having two assessors meant that there were two opinions. It also meant that the data collected has variation; however, this had minimal effect as the surveyors are specialists in their areas of expertise - i.e. archaeology or conservation. The authors attempted to limit survey bias through their respective methods of, and sparse discussion during, data collection, but there is inevitably a level of bias from previous knowledge of the storage situation, certain prominent artifacts, and/or the assessor's educational influence.

Survey fatigue must also be considered during interpretation. There were, inevitably, some mistakes made in data collection as the surveyors mainly worked in the middle of the summer for long periods of time. To reduce bias in this test, though, the surveyors did not change their assessment of the artifacts after the fact.

While the surveyors attempted to make data collection as quantitative as possible, it is qualitative in many respects. Neither the significance nor conservation data collected would have been collected with the exact same results by a different surveyor. The data must, instead, be understood as being collected through expertise, within the established framework. The assessors' professional opinions and suggestions are, therefore, included instead of avoiding opinion in favor of purely quantitative data.

Finally, this survey was, in many ways, experimental. While there is precedent for a conservation survey of this type at the Museum (Wallace 2016, Ardrey 1996) and for significance assessments at other institutions (Dunn and Das 2009; CyMAL 2013; Reed 2018), these surveys have different objectives and scopes than this particular project. The categories and scoring rubrics in both portions of this survey should be reviewed, critiqued, and augmented for future survey work. Currently, institutional peer review is underway.

Survey Criteria

Conservation

Several condition-based assessments were performed at the Museum in the past (Wallace 2016, Ardrey 1996). While these provide valuable information, all previous assessments either focused specifically on individual object condition or gave general recommendations to improve spatial concerns. The combination of both the micro- and macro-view were not presented. By uniting these two levels of assessment, a more realistic analysis of the objects and their health is generated. This survey's conservation assessment form was designed specifically to capture as much information about the conservation situation as possible. It is not enough to know the condition of the object; one must also understand what is causing the damage in order to mitigate the issue.

The evaluation utilized existing collections assessment methodologies adapted to suit the needs of the project. The form was an amalgamation of several traditional conservation assessment tools: the condition report, the environmental assessment, and the treatment proposal. The condition section was based on the condition reporting system developed by Suzanne Keene at the Museum of London in the 1990s (Keene 1991). The other sections were constructed specifically for the survey (Fleming and Haines 2018).

Conservation Priority Qualities	Scoring
Condition: How stable is the object? Describe the type of damage present.	1 = stable 2 = unstable, slow deterioration 3 = unstable, fast deterioration 4 = unstable, rapidly deteriorating
Environment: What type of environment is the object located in and does it promote stability?	1 = adequate 2 = inadequate, but not causing damage 3 = improper, causing damage
Housing: Is the object protected by a support or enclosure? If so, does it promote stability?	1 = adequate 2 = inadequate, but not causing damage 3 = improper, causing damage
Conservation: What actions are recommended to *stabilize* the object? Briefly outline recommendations.	1 = little to no conservation necessary 2 = minor conservation necessary 3 = major conservation necessary 4 = Special Project - object requires additional consideration: dedicated funding, treatment will span several years, etc.

TABLE 1: Scoring rubric for conservation priority

Objects are scored using four criteria: object condition, environmental assessment, housing assessment, and conservation requirements (Table 1). The assessor must determine what type of damage is present and what external factors are causing the damage. An object's environment and housing are scored based on the appropriateness of the conditions to promoting stability. The assessor then gives a brief outline of the conservation needs. Each category is scored and the combined total represents the conservation score (out of 14).

In order for the four criteria to be applicable to any object; regardless of material, age, or type; stability was adopted as the standard of comparison. Objects are, therefore, not compared to each other, but rather they are compared to their "ideal" state. This benchmark is particularly important if the sample population is diverse. Specialist knowledge is also required to determine what type of deterioration has occurred and how great an impact it has on an artifact's stability. Additionally, the expert must be able to give a brief explanation of the steps required to stabilize the artifact. Therefore, it is vital that the conservator specialize in the type of collection under review. For this reason, an archaeological conservator assessed the outdoor collection.

Using the four conservation criteria, the survey population can be organized based on both the degree of degradation and the degree of action required to stabilize an object. Objects which received high conservation assessment scores on average are in advanced states of deterioration and potentially require invasive or extensive treatment. Objects with low conservation criteria are assumed to be more stable and less in need of immediate intervention; their rate of change is negligible.

However, it is not practical to organize the entire collection based on need alone. Conservation resources, like time, staff, and money, tend to be limited for many organizations. If objects are treated solely based on condition, most dire first, there is a risk that resources will be focused on less important artifacts, leaving more significant objects to deteriorate before stabilization is available. Thus, it was necessary to include significance criteria.

Significance

In order to create a system with which to quantify significance of a single artifact, and to make it comparable to other artifacts in the collection, it was necessary to make a scoring rubric which represented different indicators of significance and to ask those questions in a way that would encourage reproducible scores when carried out by different surveyors.

Initially, four categories were identified as integral to quantifying significance - rarity, relatability, "wow" factor, and provenance - each with quantitative scores.

Historic Priority Qualities	Scoring
Rarity: How many examples of this object exist in the world?	0 = 101 or more examples 1 = 21 – 100 examples 2 = 6 – 20 examples 3 = 1 - 5 examples
Audience Understanding: What level must one be at to understand the significance of this artifact to our mission statement without interpretation?	0 = it is difficult to understand the connection 1 = only an expert in maritime history could understand 2 = one must have a moderate knowledge in maritime history to understand 3 = a novice could understand.
Provenance: Can we trace the history of this artifact's ownership/burial?	0 = no 1 = partially 2 = yes
Breadth of Interest: Does this artifact's history/interpretation have a significant impact on local, national, or international history?	0 = no impact 1 = local impact 2 = national impact 3 = international impact 4 = 2 of the 3 5 = all three.
Other Examples: Are there other examples of this object in the collection in better condition? OR Does this example have features that make it unique?	0 = there are more than 5 examples in better condition in our collection 1 = there are 3-5 other examples in better condition 2 = there are 1-2 other examples in better condition 3 = this is the only example, OR this example is in the best condition, OR this example has unique features
Museum Centers of Excellence: Does this artifact better one of the Museum's Centers of Excellence (exploration, commerce, conflict, technology, inspiration, recreation)?	0 = no 1 = yes
Requests: Is this object requested for research, loan, reproduction, or exhibition purposes?	0 = no OR I don't know 1 = yes
Aesthetics, pre-interpretation: Is this artifact likely to wow or stun the audience without interpretation?	0 = no 1 = yes; it is big, shiny, or otherwise impressive
Aesthetics, post-interpretation: Is this artifact likely to wow or stun the audience after it has been explained?	0 = no 1 = maybe, it depends on the audience 2 = yes, this story is amazing!

TABLE 2: Scoring rubric for historical significance priority

These were meant to quantify significance from gathered qualitative data; like maker, date of manufacture, markings, and so on; when considering the artifact in a typological system.

Some challenges arose, like the difficulty of quickly researching entire typologies for such a diverse collection, but the initial system results were positive. Additionally, during institutional peer review, supplementary criteria were posed which expanded the significance scoring rubric from four to nine qualities, with the intent of creating a more holistic view of an object's interpretive characteristics.

These nine qualities are: rarity, audience understanding, provenance, breadth of interest, other examples, museum centers of excellence, requests, aesthetics (pre-interpretation), and aesthetics (post-interpretation) (Table 2). These include the initial four criteria, though the scoring system for "wow" factor was broken into pre- and post-interpretation aesthetics. When combined, the highest possible score is 25.

Ultimately, the higher an artifact's significance score, the more significant that artifact is; which does not mean that something with a middling score is completely insignificant. Instead, it must be looked at in comparison to similar artifacts, which will also likely have middling scores. Similarly, this scoring rubric should be used in conjunction with the conservation assessment for the best understanding of the artifact's overall priority in the museum setting.

Health and Safety

During assessment, the conservation expert is responsible for the additional task of commenting on any health and safety concerns. The inclusion of a health and safety section, separate from the priority scoring system, is part of an effort to record as much information about the current situation as possible, but should not influence the priority score.

The section draws awareness to any issues that could jeopardize the safety of staff or the collection. It is intentionally scored using letters (A-D) so that it cannot be accidentally added to the priority system. A separate health and safety score box is located at the top of the conservation assessment form. The conservation expert is the primary recorder; however, the significance expert should add any information they may be aware of, as well.

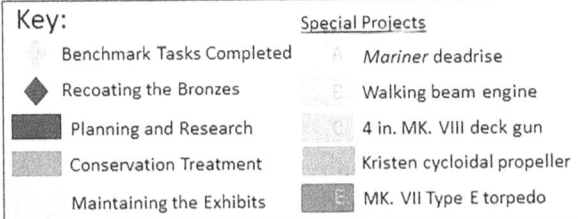

FIGURE 1: Theoretical conservation timeline based on survey results. (Author, 2018)

The health and safety assessment's purpose is not to alarm the staff, but rather draw attention to issues so that proper examination and mitigation can be scheduled. For example, three lead bilge pipes recovered in the 1930's and associated with the Siege of Yorktown, 1781, were assessed during the outdoor collection survey. Lead is a toxic material and can be dangerous if improperly handled, but these pipes come from an important archaeological site, and as such should never be discarded based on toxicity alone. As long as proper storage and handling protocols are followed, they are safe to remain in the collection.

Analytical testing using a portable Bruker Tracer III-V+ X-ray Fluorescence spectrometer (XRF) was performed during the survey for a limited number of objects. The survey presented the perfect opportunity to discuss analytical protocols within the Museum, and to test the use of the XRF unit in public spaces. However, analysis is time consuming, and it is recommended that during future assessments a list of potential threats is created for testing at a later date.

Results

The prioritization system made an overwhelming situation manageable. A total of 321 objects representing 16 artifact types, 6 collection types, 11 material types, and over 300 years of history were assessed. By creating a priority database, it was possible to focus on specific artifact groupings, compare material types, and make general statements about the entire collection.

The survey identified several collections care tasks which could be performed immediately. Staff were able to reassociate and tag the more than 100 artifacts that were missing labels. Staff were also able to remove about 30 modern intrusive materials to clearly delineate collections storage from other tasks. Additionally, 13 artifacts that were found to be triplicate or more examples of collections pieces were deaccessioned and disposed of according to the collections management policy.

The Museum is also developing new, and updating existing, policies and procedures using data from the survey. This includes questions of health and safety, access and security, and object stewardship. One of the most important groups to be discussed are the 76 artifacts on exterior display. Because of this survey, a conservation maintenance plan and schedule are in development. Additionally, the historical significance data collected can be used to identify appropriate and like artifacts to replace those objects which need to be taken off display for conservation purposes.

Arguably the most important aspect of the survey is its ability to facilitate long-range planning for conservation projects based on interpretation needs. The survey identified 42 "first priority" objects which are highly significant and deteriorating rapidly. These were noted as needing attention ahead of other objects.

Those objects with the lowest combined scores were divided into two groups - stable and significant, and unstable and insignificant. These were considered "last priority" either because they do not require intervention or the cost of conservation does not outweigh their relative significance to the Museum's mission at this time. The subtleties within the ranking system made it possible to organize the remaining bulk of the collection into groups based on condition and similar needs. Treatment order can be determined by sorting these groups further when projects begin or when additional funding is available.

To illustrate this point, a twenty year conservation timeline was constructed outlining various projects which need to occur for the outdoor collection - both individual treatments and generalized collections care actions (Figure 1). This is purely theoretical due to the Museum's many other responsibilities; however, this represents the ability for assessors to look at an assemblage and determine what actions need to occur and to structure a response based on need, funding, or other qualifiers.

The opportunity to employ the results of the survey within a real application arose a few months after the assessment took place. A 3,000 square foot, non-climate controlled building, previously used for boat building demonstrations, became available for object storage. Since the artifacts surveyed needed to be moved most pressingly for conservation reasons, surveyors organized the database to reflect conservation need, most highly in this case. That meant that those artifacts which would lose more than ten percent of their surface material in the next year were first considered to go inside. Additional qualities like presence of mechanical parts, organic materials, and other characteristics that would affect stability, were then considered. Next, those artifacts that were highly significant to the collection were considered. Finally, artifacts were considered based solely on size as surveyors tried to fill every inch of the new space. In all, 148 objects were moved to indoor storage.

The remaining, and most stable, artifacts were then reorganized on an exterior concrete pad. This will prevent them from becoming further buried in the ground and will ensure that they are no longer confused with modern intrusive items. These will soon be covered with a vinyl tarp system to prevent further light and water damage.

The relocation and reorganization of the outdoor collection succeeded in part due to the survey's prioritization system. It is possible, that if this system was not utilized, objects would have been chosen for relocation based on a generic plan; for example, sweeping the outdoor area left to right; thereby overlooking those objects most in need of covered storage.

The scoring system does not, however, replace common sense decision making; rather it provides quantitative, statistical data to help guide and justify the decision making process. For example, some artifacts were simply too large or too heavy to move into the new space even though they were highly significant and/or in need of conservation. Therefore, the next suitable artifact was considered instead. Similarly, some artifacts ranked highly in conservation and low in significance, giving them an overall middling score. Because of this, many arose as potential candidates for the move. In this case, discussion about their insignificance to the Museum's mission played heavily into the decision to leave them outside, and in most cases, to deaccession them entirely. Here, discussion and common sense decision making were integral in creating the best plan for relocation.

Finally, institutional review of the system is allowing the Museum to adapt the survey for different collections, including objects in the general collection, USS *Monitor* archaeological collection, and the Museum's Library and Archives. These projects will help the institution understand more fully the significance, breath, and health of their resources and holdings. Currently, plans are in process for projects within the Library and the general objects collection.

Peer critique has also proven useful. Two teams of experts were created among staff members, one focused on significance and the other on conservation. The teams reviewed the forms and provided feedback on form completeness and clarity. As discussed earlier, the significance score expanded from four criteria to nine based on staff discussions. The conservation assessment retained its original four categories; however, conservators worked together to clarify language and add/subtract fields as necessary. The health and safety section was greatly altered as well to reflect the diversity of potential hazards within the Museum's holdings.

After completion of the survey, several United Kingdom based significance assessment systems were found. These have varying criteria and scoring rubrics; but most focused on assessment of collections, not specific artifacts. Additionally, these systems require the participation of multiple staff members, rather than two specialists (Dunn and Das 2009; CyMAL 2013; Reed 2018). These will be analyzed and utilized in review and critique of the Museum's system, too.

The next step will be testing the system for reproducibility and legibility among various experts using the system on other collection types. The ultimate goal is to create a model that is applicable throughout the Museum and which can be adapted to other cultural heritage institutions and projects. Practice of this model will benefit future curation and exhibit goals, organize preventive care, and streamline conservation planning by considering conservation and significance together.

Conclusion

In conclusion, a survey system of this nature has many benefits. Combining significance and condition criteria present a more holistic view of an artifact. Collections care decisions will be influenced not just by the needs of objects, but also by their relative significance. Additional benefits include: producing updated inventories of collections spaces, and assisting with collection consolidation, spatial organization, and rehousing projects.

Curatorial decisions which focus on the significance of objects will be supported by conservation needs, too. The survey identifies areas of significance within collections and places importance on those artifacts. When combined with the conservation score, this information will facilitate loan and exhibition planning by narrowing down possible candidates, first by significance within the chosen theme, and then, further, by the amount of conservation required to prepare objects for use.

The priority system will also lead to better long-range planning as an institution. It can be used to garner support and secure funding for collections conservation, additional acquisitions, or exhibitions. The data can also generate lists of potential projects which would provide excellent internship or fellowship opportunities, or possible higher education research topics. Additionally, it can help improve institutional health and safety protocols by identifying concerns which need to be addressed.

As this survey system still needs revision, please contact the authors with any questions or comments, or for copies of the forms. Once the forms are fully reviewed and established within The Mariners' Museum and Park, we hope to work with other groups in order to test the system on a larger scale.

References

ARDREY, ELIZABETH D.
1996 The Mariners' Museum General Conservation Survey 1996. Manuscript, The Mariners' Museum and Park, Newport News, VA.

CYMAL (MUSEUMS LIBRARIES AND ARCHIVES WALES)
2013 *Why Do We Have It? A Significance Process and Template.* Llywodraeth Cymru (Welsh Government) < https://gweddill.gov.wales/docs/drah/publications/130327significanceen.pdf>. Accessed 25 April 2019.

DUNN, JAYNE AND SUBHADRA DAS
[2009] *The UCL Collections Review Toolkit.* UCL Culture, University College London <https://www.ucl.ac.uk/culture/resources?nid=781>. Accessed 25 April 2019.

FLEMING, HANNAH AND LESLEY HAINES
2018 The Mariners' Museum and Park Outdoor Collection Survey - 2017. Manuscript, The Mariners' Museum and Park, Newport News, VA.

KEENE, SUZANNE
1991 Audits of Care: a Framework for Collections Condition Surveys. In *Storage, Papers given at a UKIC conference Restoration '91, London 1991*, Mark Norman and Victoria Todd, editors, pp. 6-16. The United Kingdom Institute for Conservation, London, UK.

REED, CAROLINE
2018 *Reviewing Significance 3.0.* Collections Trust <https://collectionstrust.org.uk/resource/reviewing-significance-3-0/>. Accessed 25 April 2019.

WALLACE, FREDERICK
2016 2016 General Conservation Survey. Manuscript, The Mariners' Museum and Park, Newport News, VA.

. . . .

Hannah Fleming
The Mariners' Museum and Park
100 Museum Drive
Newport News, VA 23606
W: 757-952-0465
hfleming@marinersmuseum.org

Lesley Haines
The Mariners' Museum and Park
100 Museum Drive
Newport News, VA 23606
W: 757-591-7762
lhaines@marinersmuseum.org

2020 ACUA Calendar
A Showcase of 2019 Photography Competition Winners

Category A: *Color Archaeological Site Image*
Nicole Grinnon, *Site Assessments of the steamship Madison in Troy Spring*
Florida Public Archaeology Network | First Place
Crystal Ptacek, *Site overview in the woods at Monticello*
Thomas Jefferson's Monticello, Second Place

Category B: *Color Archaeological Field Work*
Mark Kostro, *Screens, Robert Carter House, Williamsburg, VA*
Colonial Williamsburg | First Place
Stephen James, *I love my job, it is my chosen profession*
PanAmerican Consultants | Second Place
Eric Larson, *Excavations of Alexander Spostwood's 1720s Enchanted Castle*
Germania Foundation | People's Choice

Category C: *Archaeological Lab Work*
Sierra Medellin, *Elevations Underground Archaeology beneath Mount Vernon*
Mount Vernon | First Place, People's Choice

Category D: *Color Artifact*
Katherine Boyle, *Fine Finish*
University of Maryland | First Place, People's Choice

Advisory Council on Underwater Archaeology

Category D: *Color Artifact*
Sierra Medellin, *Waiting for Discovery: A wine bottle in South Grove*
Mount Vernon | Second Place

Category E: *Black & White Image*
Mark Kostro, *Bee Stopper*
Colonial Williamsburg Foundation | First Place, People's Choice

Category F: *Color Archaeological Portraits*
Sierra Medellin, *Backfill by the Potomac: Alice Keith at work in South Grove*
Mount Vernon | First Place
Brandon Herrmann, *UWF – No Limits, Pensacola, Florida*
University of West Florida | People's Choice

Category G: *Diversity*
No Entry

Category H: *Artist's Perspective*
Lily Carhart, *Remains of 1880s Furnace in the cellar of George Washington's Mt. Vernon*
Mt. Vernon | First Place
Samantha Ellens, *Worked Bottle Base* Unaffiliated | Second Place

www.ingramcontent.com/pod-product-compliance
Lightning Source LLC
Chambersburg PA
CBHW081500070526
44586CB00019B/2438